Gregg Shorthand

GREGG PUBLISHING DIVISION

Dictionary Simplified

A DICTIONARY OF 30,000 AUTHORITATIVE
GREGG SHORTHAND OUTLINES

John Robert Gregg

Louis A. Leslie

Charles E. Zoubek

McGraw-Hill Book Company, Inc.
New York   Chicago   San Francisco   Dallas   Toronto   London

GREGG SHORTHAND DICTIONARY SIMPLIFIED

Copyright, 1949, by The Gregg Publishing Company. Copyrighted in the United States of America, Great Britain and Ireland, France, Italy, and Spain. All rights reserved. This book, or parts thereof, may not be reproduced in any form without permission of the publishers. Philippines Copyright, 1951, by The Gregg Publishing Company
(Act 3134, secs. 11 and 16.)
Code No. 24547 Text
Code No. 24545 Trade

Nov. 1952-NP-50

Shorthand Plates Written by
CHARLES RADER

PUBLISHED BY GREGG PUBLISHING DIVISION
McGraw-Hill Book Company, Inc.
Printed in the United States of America

FOREWORD

This shorthand dictionary is divided into three parts:

Part One contains, in alphabetic order, the shorthand outlines for 26,098 words. These 26,098 words, however, represent a considerably larger vocabulary, as many simple derivatives—those ending in *-ing* and *-s,* for example, which present no stenographic problem—have been omitted.

Part Two contains, in alphabetic order, the shorthand outlines for 2,604 entries for personal and geographical names.

Part Three consists of a list of 72 shorthand outlines for abbreviations such as *f.o.b.* and *C.O.D.*

It is easily possible to construct briefer outlines for many of the scientific and literary words for which full outlines are given in this dictionary. It is not advisable to do so, however, unless the writer is certain that he will use those briefer outlines with sufficient frequency to justify the effort of learning them. Otherwise, the brief but half-remembered outline will cause mental hesitation that will result in slower rather than faster writing.

The experience of expert shorthand writers of every system is conclusive in establishing the inadvisability of attempting to gain speed by devising and learning lists of brief outlines. Longer outlines that are quickly constructed by the mind under pressure of dictation give the writer more speed; the attempt to remember and use large numbers of abbreviated outlines tends to reduce the writer's speed.

It is hoped that this volume will render a useful service to the shorthand writer by placing at his disposal a facile and fluent outline for any word in which he may be interested.

The Publishers

PART ONE

Part One of this dictionary contains 26,098 word entries alphabetically arranged.

Experience has proved that those using a shorthand dictionary often consult it for the simple words formerly omitted from shorthand dictionaries or for rare and unusual words likewise formerly omitted.

The present list, therefore, includes many of the apparently simple words formerly omitted. It includes many of the simple derivatives formerly omitted. Most readily apparent will be the addition of the many rare and unusual words that experience has proved are wanted by users of such a list as this.

Many words are included because the shorthand learner, while still in school, has occasion to use them in his schoolwork. For this reason, many mathematical, mineralogical, chemical, physical, botanical, and physiological terms are included. For the same reason, many literary words are included, words that are of no business value but that the high school or college learner uses in schoolwork. The bulk of the vocabulary, however, consists of words used in business-office dictation.

Consistency, rather than brevity of outline, has been the guiding principle in the construction of the shorthand outlines in this *Gregg Shorthand Dictionary Simplified*. The fastest shorthand outline (within reasonable limits) is the outline that requires the least mental effort, the outline that is written consistently and analogically. The speed of a shorthand outline is not to be judged by its brevity to the eye, nor even by its facility for the hand; it is to be judged by the speed with which it may be constructed by the mind and supplied by the mind to the hand.

A

abacus	abed	abode
abaft	aberration	abolish
abalone	abet	abolition
abandon	abetted	abolitionist
abandoned	abettor	abominable
abandonment	abeyance	abominate
abase	abhor	abomination
abasement	abhorred	aboriginal
abash	abhorrence	aborigines
abatable	abhorrent	abortive
abate	abide	abound
abated	ability	aboundingly
abatement	abject	about
abbess	abjuration	above
abbey	abjure	abrade
abbot	abjured	abraded
abbreviate	ablative	abrasion
abbreviated	ablaze	abrasive
abbreviation	able	abreast
abdicate	ablest	abridge
abdicated	ablution	abridged
abdication	ably	abridgment
abdomen	abnegation	abroad
abdominal	abnormal	abrogate
abduct	abnormality	abrogated
abducted	abnormity	abrogation
abduction	aboard	abrupt

1

abscess	abstract	accelerate
abscissa	abstracted	accelerated
abscond	abstractedly	acceleration
absconded	abstraction	accelerative
absconder	abstractly	accelerator
absence	abstruse	accent
absent	absurd	accented
absentee	absurdity	accentuate
absently	absurdly	accentuation
absinth	abundance	accept
absolute	abundant	acceptability
absolutely	abuse	acceptable
absolution	abused	acceptance
absolutism	abusive	acceptation
absolutist	abusively	access
absolve	abusiveness	accessibility
absorb	abut	accessible
absorbed	abutment	accession
absorbent	abutter	accessory
absorbingly	abysm	accidence
absorption	abysmal	accident
absorptive	abyss	accidental
abstain	acacia	accidentally
abstained	academic	accipitrine
abstainer	academician	acclaim
abstemious	academies	acclaimed
abstemiously	academy	acclamation
abstemiousness	Acadian	acclamatory
abstention	acanthus	acclimate
abstinence	accede	acclimated
abstinent	acceded	acclimation

2

acclimatization accouterment achieve
acclimatize accredit achieved
acclimatized accredited achievement
acclivity accretion achromatic
accolade accrual achromatosis
accommodate accrue acid
accommodated accrued acidification
accommodatingly accumulate acidify
accommodation accumulated acidity
accommodative accumulates acidly
accompaniment accumulation acidosis
accompanist accumulative acidulate
accompany accumulator acidulous
accomplice accuracy acknowledge
accomplish accurate acknowledged
accomplished accurately acknowledgment
accomplishment accusation acme
accord accusative acne
accordance accuse acolyte
accorded accused aconite
accordingly accuser acorn
accordion accustom acoustic
accost accustomed acoustical
accosted ace acoustics
account acerb acquaint
accountability acerbity acquaintance
accountable acetate acquaintanceship
accountancy acetic acquainted
accountant acetone acquiesce
accounted acetylene acquiescence
accoutered ache acquiescent

3

acquire	actor	addicted
acquirement	actress	addiction
acquires	actual	addition
acquisition	actualities	additional
acquisitive	actuality	additionally
acquisitiveness	actually	additive
acquit	actuary	address
acquittal	actuate	addressed
acquitted	actuated	addressee
acre	acuity	addressograph
acreage	acumen	adduce
acrid	acute	adduct
acridity	acutely	adduction
acrimonious	acuteness	adductive
acrimoniously	adage	adductor
acrimony	adagio	adenoid
acrobat	adamant	adenology
acrobatic	adamantine	adenoma
acropolis	adapt	adept
across	adaptability	adequacy
acrostic	adaptable	adequately
act	adaptation	adhere
acted	adapted	adhered
actinic	adapter	adherence
actinium	adaptive	adherent
action	add	adhesion
actionable	added	adhesive
activate	addenda	adieu
active	addendum	adipose
activities	adder	adjacency
activity	addict	adjacent

4

adjective	admirable	adorn
adjoin	admirably	adorned
adjoined	admiral	adornment
adjourn	admiralty	adrenal
adjourned	admiration	adrenaline
adjournment	admire	adrift
adjudge	admired	adroit
adjudged	admissibility	adroitly
adjudicate	admissible	adsorption
adjudicated	admission	adulation
adjudication	admit	adulatory
adjudicator	admittance	adult
adjunct	admitted	adulterant
adjuration	admittedly	adulterate
adjuratory	admixture	adulterated
adjure	admonish	adulteration
adjured	admonished	adulterer
adjust	admonition	adulterous
adjustable	admonitory	adultery
adjusted	adobe	adumbrate
adjuster	adolescence	adumbration
adjustment	adolescent	advance
adjutancy	adopt	advanced
adjutant	adopted	advancement
administer	adoption	advantage
administered	adoptive	advantageous
administration	adorable	advent
administrative	adoration	adventitious
administratively	adore	adventure
administrator	adored	adventurer
administratrix	adoringly	adventuresome

5

adventuress	aerated	affix
adventurous	aeration	affixed
adverb	aerial	afflatus
adverbial	aerie	afflict
adverbially	aeronautical	afflicted
adversary	affability	affliction
adversative	affable	affluence
adverse	affably	affluent
adversely	affair	afford
adversity	affect	afforded
advert	affectation	affray
advertise	affected	affright
advertised	affectedly	affront
advertisement	affectingly	affronted
advice	affection	afghan
advisability	affectionate	afield
advisable	affectionately	afire
advisably	affiance	aflame
advise	affianced	afloat
advised	affiant	afoot
advisedly	affidavit	aforementioned
advisement	affiliate	aforesaid
advisory	affiliated	aforetime
advocacy	affiliation	afoul
advocate	affinity	afraid
advowson	affirm	afresh
adz	affirmation	after
aegis	affirmative	afterdeck
Aeolian	affirmatory	after-dinner
aeon	affirmed	aftereffect
aerate	affirmingly	afterglow

6

afterlife	aggravation	ague
aftermath	aggregate	ahead
afternoon	aggregation	ahoy
aftertaste	aggression	ahungered
afterthought	aggressive	aid
afterward	aggressor	aided
again	aggrieved	aigrette
against	aghast	aiguillette
agape	agile	ail
agate	agilely	ailanthus
agateware	agility	ailed
agave	agio	aileron
age	agitate	ailment
aged	agitated	aim
ageless	agitation	aimless
agency	agitator	air
agenda	agnate	aired
agendum	agnostic	airily
agent	agnosticism	airship
ageratum	agonize	airway
agglomerate	agonizingly	airy
agglomeration	agony	aisle
agglomerative	agrarian	ajar
agglutinate	agree	akimbo
agglutination	agreeability	alabaster
agglutinative	agreeable	alacrity
aggrandize	agreed	alamo
aggrandizement	agreement	alarm
aggravate	agricultural	alarmed
aggravated	agriculture	alarmingly
aggravatingly	agronomy	alarmist

7

alas	alimentary	allocation
albatross	alimony	allocution
albino	aliquot	allopath
album	alive	allopathy
albumin	alizarin	allot
albuminous	alkali	allotment
alchemy	alkalinity	allotted
alcohol	all	allow
alcoholic	allay	allowable
alcoholism	allegation	allowance
alcove	allege	alloy
alder	alleged	alloyed
alderman	allegedly	allspice
aldermanic	allegiance	allude
aleatory	allegorical	alluded
alembic	allegory	allure
alert	allergic	allured
alertly	allergy	alluringly
alexandrite	alleviate	allusion
alfalfa	alleviated	allusive
algebra	alleviation	allusively
alias	alley	alluvial
alibi	alleyway	ally
alien	alliance	almanac
alienable	allied	almighty
alienate	alligator	almond
alienation	alliteration	almoner
alienist	alliterative	almost
alight	alliteratively	alms
alignment	allocate	almshouse
alike	allocated	aloe

8

aloft	altruism	ambiguous
aloha	altruist	ambition
alone	altruistic	ambitious
along	alum	ambitiously
aloof	aluminate	amble
aloofly	aluminum	ambrosia
alopecia	alumni	ambrosial
aloud	alumnus	ambulance
alpaca	alveolus	ambulatory
alphabet	always	ambuscade
alphabetic	alyssum	ambush
alphabetical	amalgamate	ameliorate
alphabetize	amalgamated	ameliorated
already	amalgamation	ameliorative
also	amanuensis	amen
altar	amaranth	amenable
altarpiece	amass	amend
alter	amateur	amended
alterable	amateurish	amendment
alteration	amative	amends
alterative	amatory	amenity
altercation	amaze	American
alternate	amazed	Americanization
alternated	amazingly	Americanize
alternation	Amazon	amethyst
alternative	ambassador	amiability
alternator	ambassadorial	amiable
although	amber	amicable
altitude	ambidextrous	amidships
alto	ambient	amiss
altogether	ambiguity	amity

ammonia	amputate	anastigmatic
ammonium	amputated	anathematize
ammunition	amputation	anatomic
amnesia	amuck	anatomical
amnesty	amulet	anatomist
amoeba	amulets	anatomize
among	amuse	anatomy
amongst	amused	ancestor
amorous	amusement	ancestral
amorously	amusingly	ancestry
amorphous	anachronism	anchor
amortization	anachronistic	anchorage
amortize	anachronous	anchored
amortized	anaconda	anchorite
amount	anagram	anchovy
amounted	analects	ancient
amour	analgesia	ancillary
amperage	analgesic	and
ampersand	analogical	andante
amphibian	analogous	andiron
amphibious	analogy	anecdote
amphibiously	analysis	anemia
amphitheater	analyst	anemometer
amphora	analytic	anemone
ample	analytical	anent
amplification	analytically	anesthesia
amplifier	analyze	anesthetic
amplify	anarchical	anesthetize
amplitude	anarchism	angel
amply	anarchist	angelic
ampulla	anarchy	Angelus

10

anger	annihilate	anomaly
angered	annihilated	anon
angle	annihilation	anonymity
angled	anniversary	anonymous
angler	annotate	anopheles
Anglo-Saxon	annotated	another
angrily	annotation	answer
angry	announce	answerable
anguish	announced	answered
angular	announcement	ant
angularity	announcer	antagonism
aniline	annoy	antagonist
animadversion	annoyance	antagonistic
animal	annoyed	antagonize
animate	annoyingly	antagonized
animated	annual	antarctic
animatedly	annually	ante
animation	annuitant	anteater
animator	annuity	antecedent
animosity	annul	antechamber
animus	annular	antedate
anise	annulled	antelope
ankle	annulment	antenatal
anklet	annunciation	antenna
ankylosis	annunciator	anterior
annalist	anode	anteroom
annals	anodyne	anthem
anneal	anoint	anthologist
annealed	anointed	anthology
annex	anomalies	anthracite
annexation	anomalous	anthrax

11

anthropoid	anxious	apologist
anthropological	any	apologize
anthropology	anybody	apologized
antic	anyhow	apology
anticipate	anyone	apoplectic
anticipated	anything	apoplexy
anticipation	anyway	apostasy
anticipatory	anywhere	apostate
anticlimax	aorta	apostle
antidote	aortic	apostolic
antimony	apart	apostrophe
antinomy	apartment	apostrophize
antipathy	apathetic	apothecary
antiphonal	apathetically	apothegm
antipodes	apathy	apotheosis
antiquarian	aperient	appall
antiquary	aperitive	appalled
antiquated	aperture	appallingly
antique	apex	appanage
antiquity	aphasia	apparatus
antisepsis	aphid	apparel
antiseptic	aphorism	apparent
antithesis	aphoristic	apparition
antithetical	apiary	appeal
antitoxin	apical	appealed
antler	apices	appealingly
antlered	apiece	appear
antonym	apocalypse	appearance
antrum	apogee	appeared
anvil	apologetic	appeasable
anxiety	apological	appease

appeased	applicant	apprenticed
appeasement	application	apprenticeship
appeasingly	applicator	apprise
appellant	applied	apprised
appellate	apply	approach
appellation	appoint	approachable
appellee	appointed	approached
append	appointee	approbation
appendage	appointive	appropriate
appendectomy	appointment	appropriately
appended	apportion	appropriateness
appendicitis	apportioned	appropriation
appendix	apportionment	approval
appendixes	apposite	approve
apperceive	apposition	approved
apperceived	appraisal	approvingly
apperception	appraise	approximate
apperceptive	appraised	approximately
appertain	appraisingly	approximation
appertained	appreciable	appurtenance
appetite	appreciably	appurtenant
appetizer	appreciate	apricot
appetizingly	appreciated	April
applaud	appreciation	apron
applauded	appreciative	apropos
applause	appreciatively	apse
apple	apprehend	apt
applejack	apprehended	aptitude
appliance	apprehension	aptly
applicability	apprehensive	aptness
applicable	apprentice	aquamarine

13

aquarium	archduchess	argumentation
aquatic	archduchy	argumentative
aqueduct	archduke	argyrol
aqueous	archeology	arid
aquiline	archer	aridity
Arab	archery	arise
arabesque	archetype	aristocracy
Arabian	archipelago	aristocrat
Arabic	architect	aristocratic
arable	architectonic	arithmetic
arbiter	architectural	arithmetical
arbitrage	archives	ark
arbitrament	archivist	arm
arbitrarily	archly	armada
arbitrariness	archway	armadillo
arbitrary	arctic	armament
arbitrated	ardent	armature
arbitration	ardently	armchair
arbitrator	ardor	armed
arbor	arduous	Armenian
arboreal	arduously	armful
arboretum	are	armistice
arbutus	area	armlet
arc	arena	armor
arcade	argent	armorial
arcanum	argentiferous	armory
arch	argon	armpit
archaic	Argonaut	armscye
archangel	arguable	army
archbishop	argue	arnica
archdeacon	argument	aroma

aromatic	artful	ascribe
arouse	artfully	ascribed
arpeggio	arthritis	ascription
arraign	artichoke	asepsis
arraignment	article	aseptic
arrange	articulate	ash
arranged	articulated	ashamed
arrangement	articulation	ashen
arras	artifact	ashes
array	artifice	ashlar
arrearage	artificial	ashore
arrears	artificiality	ashy
arrest	artificially	Asiatic
arrival	artillery	aside
arrive	artist	asinine
arrogance	artistic	ask
arrogant	artistry	askance
arrogate	artless	askew
arrowhead	Aryan	aslant
arrowy	as	asleep
arroyo	asbestos	asp
arsenal	ascend	asparagus
arsenate	ascendant	aspect
arsenic	ascendency	aspen
arsenical	ascension	asperity
arsenide	ascent	aspersion
arsenite	ascertain	asphalt
arson	ascertainment	asphodel
art	ascetic	asphyxiate
arterial	asceticism	asphyxiation
artery	ascorbic	aspic

aspirant	assessor	assumed
aspirate	asset	assumpsit
aspiration	asseverate	assumption
aspire	asseveration	assurance
aspired	assiduity	assure
aspirin	assiduous	assured
assagai	assiduously	assuredly
assailant	assign	Assyrian
assassin	assignable	aster
assassinate	assigned	asterisk
assassinated	assignee	astern
assassination	assignment	asteroid
assault	assignor	asthenia
assaulted	assimilate	asthma
assay	assimilated	asthmatic
assayed	assimilation	astigmatic
assemblage	assist	astigmatism
assemble	assistance	astonish
assembly	assistant	astonishingly
assent	assisted	astonishment
assented	assists	astound
assentingly	associate	astoundingly
assert	associated	astragalus
asserted	association	astrakhan
assertion	associative	astral
assertive	assorted	astray
assertively	assortment	astride
assess	assuage	astringency
assessable	assuaged	astringent
assessed	assumably	astrologer
assessment	assume	astrology

astronomer	atonement	attest
astronomical	atrium	attestation
astronomy	atrocious	attests
astute	atrociously	attic
astutely	atrocity	attire
astuteness	atrophied	attired
asunder	atrophy	attitude
asylum	atropine	attitudinize
asymmetric	attach	attorney
asymmetrical	attached	attract
at	attachment	attracted
atavism	attack	attraction
atheism	attacker	attractive
atheist	attain	attractively
atheistic	attainable	attribute
atheneum	attainder	attribution
Athenian	attained	attributive
athlete	attainment	attrition
athletic	attar	auburn
athletics	attempt	auction
athwart	attempted	auctioneer
atmosphere	attend	audacious
atmospheric	attendance	audaciously
atoll	attendant	audacity
atom	attention	audibility
atomic	attentive	audible
atomize	attentively	audibly
atomized	attentiveness	audience
atomizer	attenuate	audit
atone	attenuated	audited
atoned	attenuation	audition

auditor	Austrian	availability
auditorium	authentic	available
auditory	authenticate	availed
auger	authentication	avalanche
aught	authenticity	avarice
augment	author	avaricious
augmentation	authoritarian	avariciously
augmentative	authoritative	avatar
augur	authority	avenge
augured	authorization	avenged
augury	authorize	avenue
august	authorized	aver
August	authorship	average
augustly	autobiography	averred
auk	autochthonous	averse
aunt	autocracy	aversion
aura	autocrat	avert
aureole	autocratic	averted
auricle	autograph	aviary
auricular	automatic	aviation
auriferous	automatism	aviator
aurora	automaton	avid
auroral	automobile	avidity
auscultate	autonomous	avidly
auscultation	autonomy	avigation
auspices	autopsy	avocado
auspicious	autosuggestion	avocation
austere	autumn	avoid
austerely	autumnal	avoidable
austerity	auxiliary	avowal
Australian	avail	avowedly

18

avuncular	awash	awoke
await	away	ax
awaited	awestricken	axiom
awake	awestruck	axiomatic
awaken	awful	axis
awakened	awkward	axle
award	awkwardly	azalea
awarded	awkwardness	azimuth
aware	awl	azure
awareness	awning	azurite

B

babbitt
baboon
baby
baccalaureate
bacchanal
bachelor
bachelorhood
back
backboard
backbone
backer
backfire
backgammon
background
backhand
backhanded
backlash
backlog
backslide
backwardness
backwash
backwater
bacon
bacteria
bacterial
bacteriological
bacteriology

bad
badger
badinage
badly
badminton
badness
baffle
baffled
bag
bagged
bagasse
bagatelle
baggage
bagpipe
bail
bailed
bailiff
bailiwick
bailment
bait
baize
bake
bakelite
baker
bakery
balance
balbriggan

balcony
bald
baldachin
baldric
bale
baled
baleful
balk
ball
ballad
ballast
ballerina
ballet
ballistics
balloon
balloonist
ballot
ballroom
balm
balsam
balsamiferous
baluster
balustrade
bamboo
bamboozle
bamboozled
ban

banal	banquet	bareness
banality	banshee	bargain
banana	bantam	bargained
band	banter	barge
bandage	bantered	bargeman
bandanna	banteringly	baritone
bandbox	banyan	barium
bandeau	baptism	bark
banded	baptismal	barley
bandit	Baptist	barn
banditti	baptize	barnacle
bandmaster	baptized	barogram
bandoleer	bar	barograph
bandy	barb	barometer
baneful	barbarian	barometric
bang	barbaric	baron
bangboard	barbarism	baroness
banged	barbarity	baronet
bangle	barbarous	baronetcy
banish	barbecue	baronial
banishment	barbed	baroque
banister	barber	barrack
banjo	barberry	barracuda
bank	barbican	barrage
bankbook	bard	barratry
banked	bare	barrel
banker	bareback	barren
bankrupt	bared	barrenness
bankruptcy	barefaced	barricade
banned	bareheaded	barrier
banner	barely	barrister

barrow	bastion	beaker
barter	bat	beam
bartered	batch	beamed
basal	bateau	bean
bascule	bath	bear
base	bather	bearable
baseboard	bathhouse	beard
baseless	bathos	bearded
basely	baton	bearskin
baseman	battalion	beast
basement	batter	beastliness
baseness	battered	beastly
baser	battery	beat
basest	battle	beaten
bashful	battled	beater
basic	battleship	beatific
basically	bawl	beatification
basilica	bawled	beatify
basilisk	bayberry	beatings
basin	bayonet	beatitude
basis	bayou	beau
bask	bazaar	beauteous
basket	be	beautiful
bas-relief	beach	beautifully
bass	beacon	beautify
bassinet	bead	beauty
basso	beaded	beaver
bassoon	beadle	becalm
basswood	beadwork	became
baste	beagle	because
bastinado	beak	beckon

22

beckoned	beforehand	belfry
becloud	befriend	Belgian
become	befuddle	belie
becomingly	beg	belief
bed	beget	believable
bedbug	beggar	believe
bedchamber	begged	belittle
bedeck	begin	belittled
bedevil	begone	belittlingly
bedfellow	begonia	bell
bedizen	begot	belladonna
bedlam	begrime	bellboy
bedpost	beguil	bellicose
bedridden	beguiled	bellicosity
bedroom	begun	belligerence
bedside	behalf	belligerency
bedspread	behave	belligerent
bedspring	behavior	belligerently
bedstead	behead	bellows
bedtime	beheadings	belong
bee	beheld	belonged
beech	behemoth	belongings
beef	behest	beloved
beefsteak	behind	below
beer	behold	belt
beeswax	beholden	belted
beetle	beholder	belvedere
befall	beige	bemused
befit	bejewel	bench
befog	belch	bend
before	beleaguered	bended

23

beneath
benediction
benefaction
benefactor
benefactress
benefice
beneficence
beneficent
beneficial
beneficiary
benefit
benevolence
benevolent
benighted
benignancy
benignant
benignity
bent
benzene
bequeath
bequest
bereave
bereaved
berry
berth
beryl
beseech
beseeched
beseechingly
beset
beside

besides
besiege
bespangle
bespeak
Bessemer
best
bestial
bestiality
bestow
bestowed
bestride
bet
betake
betimes
betrayal
betrayer
betroth
betrothal
better
bettered
betterment
between
betwixt
bevel
beveled
beverage
bevy
bewail
bewailed
beware
bewilder

bewildered
bewilderment
bewitch
beyond
bezel
biannual
biannually
bias
biased
bibelot
Bible
Biblical
bibliographical
bibliography
bibulous
bicameral
bicarbonate
bicentenary
biceps
bichloride
bichromate
bicuspid
bicycle
bid
bidder
bide
biennial
bier
bifocal
big
bigamist

24

bigamous	bimetallist	birthright
bigamy	bimonthly	biscuit
bigger	binary	bisect
biggest	binder	bishop
bighorn	bindery	bishopric
bight	bindingly	bismuth
bigot	bindings	bison
bigoted	bindweed	bisque
bigotry	binnacle	bit
bijou	binocular	bite
bilateral	binomial	biter
bile	biographer	bitingly
bilge	biographic	bitten
biliary	biographical	bitter
bilingual	biographically	bitterly
bilious	biography	bittern
bilk	biological	bitterness
bill	biologically	bitters
billboard	biologist	bitumen
billed	biology	bituminous
billhead	biopsy	bivouac
billiards	biplane	bizarre
billings	bipolar	black
billion	birch	blackball
billionaire	bird	blackberry
billow	birdlime	blackbird
billowy	birdman	blackboard
billposter	birth	blacken
billsticker	birthday	blacker
bimetallic	birthmark	blackest
bimetallism	birthplace	blackfish

25

blackhead	blatant	blistered
blackish	blaze	blisteringly
blackjack	blazer	blistery
blackmail	blazon	blithe
blackness	bleach	blithely
blacksmith	bleacher	blithesome
bladder	bleak	blizzard
blade	bleat	bloat
blame	bleed	block
blamed	blemish	blockade
blameless	blench	blockhead
blameworthy	blend	blockhouse
blanch	blended	blond
bland	blendings	blood
blandish	bless	blooded
blandly	blessedness	bloodier
blandness	blessings	bloodiest
blank	blew	bloodless
blanker	blight	bloodletting
blankest	blimp	bloodroot
blanket	blind	bloodshed
blankly	blinded	bloodshot
blare	blinder	bloodstain
blared	blindfold	bloody
blarney	blindly	bloom
blaspheme	blink	bloomed
blasphemed	blinker	bloomer
blasphemous	bliss	blossom
blasphemy	blissful	blossomed
blast	blissfully	blot
blasted	blister	blotch

26

blotter	blustered	bola
blouse	blusteringly	bold
blow	boa	boldly
blower	boar	boldness
blowfish	board	bolero
blowgun	boarded	boll
blowhole	boarder	bolo
blown	boast	bolometer
blowpipe	boaster	bolster
blowtorch	boastful	bolstered
blowy	boastfully	bolt
blubber	boat	bolted
bludgeon	boatswain	bolthead
blue	bobbin	bolus
bluefish	bobolink	bomb
bluestocking	bobtail	bombard
bluff	bode	bombarded
blunder	bodice	bombardier
blunderbuss	bodily	bombard-ment
blundered	bodkin	bombast
blunderingly	body	bombastic
blunt	bog	bomber
blunted	boggle	bombings
bluntly	boggled	bombproof
bluntness	bogus	bombshell
blur	Bohemian	bonanza
blurred	boil	bonbon
blurt	boiled	bond
blush	boiler	bondage
blushingly	boisterous	bonded
bluster	boisterously	bondholder

27

bondman	boomerang	borough
bondsman	boon	borrow
bone	boorish	borrowed
boned	boost	borrowings
boneless	boosted	bosky
boneset	booster	bosom
bonfire	boot	boss
bonito	bootblack	botanic
bonnet	booted	botanical
bonus	bootee	botanist
booby	booth	botanize
boodle	bootjack	botany
book	bootleg	botch
bookbinder	bootlegger	both
bookings	bootless	bother
bookish	booty	bothersome
bookkeeper	booze	bottle
bookkeeping	boracic	bottled
booklet	borate	bottom
booklets	borax	bottomless
bookmaker	Bordeaux	bottomry
bookmark	border	botulism
bookplate	bordered	boudoir
bookrack	bore	bough
bookseller	bored	bought
bookshelf	boredom	boulder
bookshop	borer	boulevard
bookstore	boric	bounce
bookworm	borings	bouncer
boom	born	bound
boomed	boron	boundary

bounded	boysenberry	brave
bounden	brace	braver
boundless	bracelet	bravery
bounteous	bracelets	bravest
bounteously	bracket	bravo
bountiful	bracketed	brawl
bounty	brackish	brawler
bouquet	bradawl	brawny
bourgeois	brag	brazen
bout	braid	brazier
bovine	braided	breach
bow	Braille	bread
bow	brain	breadfruit
bower	brainless	breadth
bowknot	brainy	breadwinner
bowl	braise	break
bowlder	brake	breakable
bowled	brakeman	breakage
bowlegged	bramble	breakdown
bowman	bran	breakfast
bowshot	branch	breakneck
bowsprit	brand	breakwater
box	branded	breast
boxed	brandied	breastbone
boxer	brandish	breastpin
boxwood	brandy	breastplate
boy	brash	breastwork
boycott	brass	breath
boyhood	brassard	breathless
boyish	brassy	breech
boyishness	bravado	breed

29

breeder	brigand	brittle
breeze	brigandage	brittleness
brethren	brigantine	broach
breve	bright	broad
brevet	brighten	broadcast
breviary	brighter	broaden
brevier	brightest	broader
brevity	brightly	broadest
brew	brightness	broadloom
brewery	brilliance	broadly
bribe	brilliant	broadside
bribed	brilliantly	brocade
bribery	brim	brocatel
brick	brimful	broccoli
brickbat	brimstone	brochette
bricklayer	brindled	brochure
brickyard	brine	brogan
bridal	bring	brogue
bride	brink	broil
bridge	briny	broiled
bridgehead	briquette	broiler
bridle	brisk	broke
bridled	brisket	broken
brief	bristle	brokenly
briefer	bristled	broker
briefest	bristly	brokerage
briefly	Britannia	bromate
brier	Britannic	bromide
brig	British	bromine
brigade	Britisher	bronchial
brigadier	Briton	bronchitis

bronze	brute	bugle
brood	brutish	bugler
brooded	bubble	build
brooder	bubonic	builder
brook	buccal	buildings
brooklet	buccaneer	built
brooklets	buck	bulb
broom	buckboard	bulbous
broth	bucket	bulge
brother	bucketful	bulged
brotherhood	buckle	bulk
brother-in-law	buckled	bulkhead
brotherly	buckler	bulkiest
brougham	buckram	bulky
brought	bucksaw	bull
brow	buckshot	bullet
brown	buckskin	bulletin
browse	buckwheat	bullfight
bruin	bucolic	bullfinch
bruise	bud	bullfrog
bruised	budge	bullhead
bruit	budged	bullion
brunette	budget	bullish
brunt	budgetary	bullock
brush	buff	bully
brushwood	buffalo	bullyrag
brusque	buffer	bulrush
brutal	buffoon	bulwark
brutality	buffoonery	bum
brutalize	bug	bumboat
brutally	bugbear	bump

bumper	burin	butler
bumpier	burlap	butt
bumpiest	burlesque	butter
bumpkin	burly	butterball
bumpy	burn	buttercup
buna	burned	buttered
bunch	burner	butterfat
bundle	burnish	butterfly
bundled	burnt	butternut
bung	burr	butterscotch
bungalow	burro	buttery
bungle	burrow	button
bungled	bursar	buttonhole
bungler	burst	buttonholed
bunion	bury	buttress
bunker	bus	buxom
buoy	bush	buy
buoyant	bushings	buyer
buoyantly	busily	buzz
burden	business	buzzard
burdensome	businesslike	buzzer
bureau	buskin	by
bureaucracy	bust	bygone
bureaucrat	bustard	bypass
burette	bustle	bypath
burgee	bustled	byplay
burgeon	busy	by-product
burgess	busybody	Byronic
burglar	but	bystander
burglary	butcher	byway
burial	butchery	byword

32

C

cab	caffeine	caliber
cabal	cage	calibrate
cabbage	caged	calibration
cabin	cairn	calico
cabinet	caitiff	caliper
cable	cajole	calisthenics
cablegram	cajolery	calk
caboose	cake	call
cacao	cakewalk	calla
cachalot	calabash	called
cache	calamitous	caller
cachet	calamitously	calligraphy
cackle	calamity	calliope
cackled	calcification	callosity
cactus	calcify	callous
cadaver	calcimine	calloused
cadaverous	calcine	callously
caddie	calcined	callow
cadence	calcium	callowly
cadenza	calculate	callus
cadet	calculated	calm
cadmium	calculation	calmer
Cadmus	calculator	calmest
cadre	caldron	calmly
caduceus	calendar	calmness
cafe	calf	calomel
cafeteria	calfskin	caloric

33

calorie	canceled	canoe
calumniate	cancellation	canon
calumniated	cancer	canonical
calumniation	cancerous	canonicals
calumniator	candelabrum	canonize
calumny	candid	canopy
Calvary	candidacy	can't
calved	candidate	cant
calyx	candidly	cantaloupe
camber	candied	cantankerous
cambium	candle	cantata
cambric	candled	canteen
came	candlefish	canter
camel	candlelight	canticle
cameleer	candlenut	cantilever
Camelot	candlestick	cantle
cameo	candor	canto
camera	candy	canton
camomile	cane	cantor
camouflage	canine	canvas
camp	canister	caoutchouc
campaign	canker	capabilities
campanile	cankerous	capability
camper	cannery	capable
camphor	cannibal	capably
camphorate	cannibalism	capacious
campus	cannily	capacitate
can	cannon	capacitated
canal	cannonade	capacity
canary	cannoneer	cape
cancel	canny	caper

caperings	captured	cardboard
capillarity	car	cardiac
capillary	carabineer	cardinal
capital	caracole	cardiograph
capitalism	caracoled	cardiology
capitalist	carafe	carditis
capitalists	caramel	care
capitalization	caramelize	cared
capitalize	carapace	careen
capitalized	carat	careened
capitulate	caravan	career
capitulated	caravansary	careful
capitulates	caravel	carefully
capitulation	caraway	carefulness
caprice	carbide	careless
capricious	carbine	carelessly
capsize	carbohydrate	carelessness
capstan	carbolic	caress
capsule	carbon	caressingly
captain	carbonate	caret
captaincy	carbonic	carfare
caption	carboniferous	cargo
captious	carbonize	caribou
captiously	carbonized	caricature
captiousness	carborundum	caricatured
captivate	carboy	caries
captivated	carbuncle	carillon
captivation	carburetor	carminative
captive	carcass	carmine
captivity	carcinoma	carnage
capture	card	carnal

35

carnally
carnation
carnelian
carnival
carnivorous
carol
caroled
carom
caromed
carotid
carouse
caroused
carp
carpal
carpenter
carpet
carpeted
carriage
carrier
carrion
carrot
carrousel
carry
cart
cartage
carted
cartel
cartilage
cartilaginous
cartography
carton

cartoon
cartouche
cartridge
carve
carved
carver
caryatid
cascade
case
casein
casement
cash
cashed
cashier
cashmere
casino
cask
casket
cassation
cassava
casserole
cassia
cassock
cast
castanet
caste
caster
castigate
castigated
castigation
castle

castoff
castor
castrametation
casual
casually
casualty
casuist
casuistry
cataclysm
catacomb
catafalque
Catalan
catalepsy
cataleptic
catalogue
catalpa
catalysis
catalytic
catalyze
catamount
catapult
cataract
catarrh
catarrhal
catastrophe
catastrophic
Catawba
catbird
catboat
catch
catcher

catchword	causeway	celebrate
catchy	caustic	celebrated
catechism	cauterization	celebration
catechize	cauterize	celebrity
categorical	cauterized	celerity
category	cautery	celery
catenary	caution	celesta
cater	cautionary	celestial
catered	cautious	celestially
caterer	cavalcade	celibacy
caterpillar	cavalier	celibate
catfish	cavalry	cell
catgut	cave	cellar
cathedral	caveat	cellarer
catheter	cavern	cellaret
catheterize	cavernous	cellist
cathode	caviar	cello
catholic	cavil	cellophane
catholicism	cavity	cellular
catholicity	cavort	cellulitis
catnip	cayenne	celluloid
cattle	cease	cellulose
caucus	ceased	Celtic
caudal	ceaseless	cement
caught	cecum	cementation
causal	cedar	cemetery
causality	cede	cenobite
causation	ceded	cenotaph
causative	cedilla	censer
cause	ceilings	censor
causeless	celebrant	censorial

37

censorious	cerebral	chained
censorship	cerebrum	chainwork
censurable	cerement	chair
censure	ceremonial	chairman
censured	ceremonially	chaise
census	ceremonious	chalcedony
cent	ceremoniously	chalet
centaur	ceremoniousness	chalice
centenarian	ceremony	chalk
centenary	cerise	chalkiness
centennial	cerium	challenge
center	certain	challenged
centerboard	certainly	chamber
centered	certainty	chambered
centerpiece	certificate	chamberlain
centigrade	certification	chambermaid
centimeter	certify	chameleon
centipede	certiorari	chamois
central	certitude	champagne
centralization	cervical	champion
centralize	cervix	championship
centralized	cesium	chance
centrally	cessation	chanced
centrifugal	cession	chancel
centripetal	cesspool	chancellery
century	cestus	chancellor
cephalalgia	cetacean	chancery
cephalic	chafe	chandelier
ceramic	chaffinch	chandler
cereal	chagrin	chandlery
cerebellum	chain	change

changeable	charioteer	chatty
changeless	charitable	cheap
changeling	charitably	cheapen
channel	charity	cheapened
channeled	charlatan	cheaper
chant	charm	cheapest
chanted	charmed	cheaply
chaos	charmingly	cheapness
chaotic	chart	cheat
chapel	charted	cheated
chaperon	charter	check
chaplain	chartreuse	checked
chaplet	chary	checker
chaplets	chase	checkerboard
chapter	chasm	checkered
chapters	chassis	checkmate
char	chaste	checkrein
character	chasten	cheeky
characteristic	chastened	cheer
characteristically	chasteningly	cheered
characterization	chastise	cheerful
characterize	chastised	cheerfully
characterized	chastisement	cheerfulness
charade	chastity	cheerily
charcoal	chasuble	cheeringly
chard	chateau	cheerless
charge	chatelaine	cheerlessly
chargeable	chattel	cheery
charged	chatter	cheese
charger	chattered	cheesecake
chariot	chatterer	cheesecloth

39

chef	childishly	chirp
chemical	childishness	chisel
chemically	childless	chiseled
chemise	childlike	chitterling
chemist	children	chivalric
chemistry	chili	chivalrous
chemurgy	chill	chivalry
chenille	chilled	chive
cherish	chillier	chloral
cheroot	chilliest	chlorate
cherry	chillingly	chloride
cherub	chilly	chlorinate
chess	chime	chlorine
chest	chimed	chlorite
chestnut	chimera	chloroform
chevron	chimerical	chlorophyll
chew	chimney	chlorosis
chicanery	chimpanzee	chocolate
chicken	chin	choice
chicle	china	choir
chicory	chinch	choke
chide	chinchilla	choler
chief	chine	cholera
chiefly	Chinese	choleric
chieftain	chink	choose
chiffon	chintz	chop
chiffonier	chip	chophouse
chilblain	chipmunk	choral
child	chipper	chord
childhood	chirography	chorea
childish	chiropodist	chortle

chorus	chummy	circular
chose	chump	circularize
chosen	chunk	circulate
chowder	church	circulated
chrism	churchman	circulation
christen	churlish	circulatory
Christendom	churlishly	circumambient
christened	churn	circumference
christenings	churned	circumferential
Christian	chute	circumflex
Christianity	chutney	circumlocution
Christmas	cicada	circumlocutory
chromatics	cicatrix	circumnavigate
chrome	cicatrize	circumscribe
chromium	cider	circumscribed
chronic	cigar	circumspect
chronicle	cigarette	circumspection
chronicled	cinch	circumspectly
chronicles	cincture	circumspectness
chronological	cinder	circumstance
chronologically	cinematograph	circumstances
chronology	cinnamon	circumstantial
chronometer	cinquefoil	circumstantially
chrysalis	cion	circumstantiate
chrysanthemum	cipher	circumvent
chubbiness	circle	circumvention
chubby	circled	circus
chuck	circuit	cirrhosis
chuckle	circuitous	cirrhotic
chucklehead	circuitously	cistern
chum	circuitousness	citadel

citation	clamshell	clause
cite	clan	claustrophobia
cited	clandestine	clavichord
citizen	clang	clavicle
citizenry	clanged	claw
citizenship	clangor	clay
citrate	clank	clean
citric	clanked	cleaned
citron	clap	cleaner
city	clapper	cleanest
civic	claptrap	cleanliness
civil	claque	cleanly
civilian	claret	cleanness
civility	clarification	cleanse
civilization	clarify	cleanser
civilize	clarinet	clear
civilized	clarion	clearance
claim	clarity	cleared
claimant	clash	clearer
claimed	clasp	clearest
clairvoyance	class	clearly
clairvoyant	classic	clearness
clamant	classical	cleat
clambake	classicism	cleavage
clamber	classicist	cleave
clambered	classicists	cleaver
clammy	classification	clef
clamor	classify	cleft
clamored	classmate	clematis
clamorous	clatter	clemency
clamp	clattered	clement

clench	clinker	cloudy
clerestory	clip	clove
clergy	clipper	cloven
clergyman	clippings	clover
clerical	clique	clown
clerk	cloak	clowned
clever	clock	clownish
cleverer	clockwise	cloy
cleverest	clod	cloyed
cleverly	clog	club
cleverness	cloister	cluck
clew	cloistered	clump
click	clonic	clumsier
client	close	clumsiest
clientele	closed	clumsily
cliff	closely	clumsiness
climacteric	closeness	clumsy
climate	closer	cluster
climatic	closest	clustered
climax	closet	clutch
climb	closure	clutter
climbed	clot	cluttered
climber	clothe	coach
clinch	clothes	coachman
clincher	clothespin	coadjutor
cling	clothier	coagulate
clingingly	clotted	coagulated
clinic	cloud	coagulates
clinical	cloudiness	coagulation
clinician	cloudless	coagulative
clink	clouds	coal

43

coalesce	cockpit	cogitation
coalescence	cockroach	cogitative
coalescent	cocksure	cognac
coalition	cocksureness	cognate
coalsack	cocktail	cognizance
coarse	cocoa	cognizant
coarsen	cocoon	cognomen
coarsened	code	cohabit
coarser	coded	cohere
coarsest	codefendant	cohered
coast	codeine	coherence
coastal	codex	coherent
coaster	codfish	coherently
coastwise	codicil	coherer
coat	codification	cohesion
coatings	codify	cohesive
coauthor	coeducation	cohesiveness
coax	coefficient	cohort
coaxed	coerce	coif
coaxial	coerced	coiffure
coaxingly	coercion	coign
cobalt	coercive	coil
cobble	coeval	coiled
cobra	coexecutor	coin
cobweb	coffee	coinage
cocaine	coffer	coincide
coccyx	coffin	coincidence
cochineal	cogency	coincidental
cockade	cogent	coined
cockatoo	cogitate	coiner
cockney	cogitated	coinsurance

coinsure	collision	columbine
coinsurer	collocation	column
coke	collodion	columnar
colander	colloid	coma
cold	colloidal	comatose
colder	colloquial	comb
coldest	colloquy	combat
coldly	collotype	combatant
colic	collusion	combative
colitis	collusive	combed
collaborate	cologne	combination
collaboration	colon	combine
collapse	colonel	combings
collar	colonial	combust
collate	colonist	combustible
collated	colonization	combustion
collateral	colonize	come
collation	colonized	comedian
colleague	colonnade	comedy
collect	colony	comeliness
collected	colophon	comely
collectible	color	comestible
collection	coloration	comet
collective	colored	comfit
collector	colorings	comfort
college	colorless	comfortable
collegiate	colossal	comfortably
collide	Colosseum	comforted
collided	colossus	comforter
collie	colporteur	comic
collier	colt	comical

45

comings	comminatory	communicant
comma	commingle	communicate
command	commingled	communication
commandeer	comminute	communicative
commander	comminuted	communion
commandingly	comminution	communism
commandment	commiserate	communist
commando	commiseration	communistic
commemorate	commissariat	community
commemorated	commissary	communize
commemoration	commission	commutation
commemorative	commissioned	commutator
commence	commissioner	commute
commenced	commit	commuted
commencement	commitment	commuter
commend	committed	compact
commendable	committee	companion
commendation	commodious	companionable
commendatory	commodity	companionship
commended	commodore	companionway
commensurable	common	company
commensurate	commonalty	comparability
comment	commoner	comparable
commentary	commonest	comparative
commentator	commonly	compare
commented	commonplace	compared
commerce	commonwealth	comparison
commercial	commotion	compartment
commercialism	communal	compass
commercialization	commune	compassion
commercialize	communicable	compassionate

46

compassionately
compatible
compatriot
compeer
compel
compelled
compellingly
compend
compendious
compendium
compensate
compensation
compensatory
compete
competence
competent
competently
competition
competitive
competitor
compilation
compile
compiled
complacence
complacency
complacent
complain
complainant
complained
complainingly
complaint

complaisant
complement
complemental
complementary
complemented
complete
completed
completion
complex
complexion
complexity
compliance
compliant
complicate
complicated
complication
complicity
complied
compliment
complimentary
complin
comply
component
comport
compose
composed
composer
composite
composition
compositor
compost

composure
compote
compound
comprehend
comprehended
comprehensibility
comprehensible
comprehension
comprehensive
compress
compressibility
compressible
compression
compressor
comprise
compromise
compromisingly
comptometer
comptroller
compulsion
compulsory
compunction
computation
compute
computed
comrade
concatenation
concave
concavity
conceal
concealed

47

concealment	conclude	conditional
concede	concluded	conditionally
conceit	conclusion	condole
conceited	conclusive	condolence
conceitedly	conclusively	condonation
conceivable	concoct	condone
conceivably	concoction	condoned
conceive	concomitant	condor
conceived	concord	conducive
concentrate	concordance	conduct
concentration	concourse	conducted
concentric	concrete	conduction
concept	concur	conductivity
conception	concurred	conductor
conceptual	concurrence	conduit
concern	concurrent	condyle
concerned	concussion	cone
concert	condemn	confection
concerted	condemnation	confectioner
concertina	condemnatory	confectionery
concession	condemned	confederacy
concessionaire	condensation	confederate
conch	condense	confederation
conciliate	condensed	confer
conciliated	condenser	conferee
conciliation	condescend	conference
conciliatory	condescendingly	conferred
concise	condescension	confess
concisely	condign	confessedly
conciseness	condiment	confession
conclave	condition	confessional

confessor	confound	congregation
confide	confounded	congregational
confided	confrere	congress
confidence	confront	congressional
confident	confrontation	congruence
confidential	confronted	congruent
confidentially	confuse	congruity
confidently	confused	congruous
confidingly	confusedly	conic
configuration	confusingly	conical
confine	confusion	coniferous
confined	confutation	conjectural
confinement	confute	conjecture
confirm	confuted	conjectured
confirmation	congeal	conjugal
confirmed	congealed	conjugate
confiscate	congenial	conjugated
confiscated	congeniality	conjugation
confiscation	congenially	conjunction
confiscatory	congenital	conjunctive
conflagration	congest	conjunctivitis
conflict	congestion	conjuration
confliction	conglomerate	conjure
confluence	conglomeration	conjured
confluent	congratulate	conjurer
conform	congratulated	connect
conformable	congratulates	connectedly
conformation	congratulation	connecter
conformed	congratulatory	connection
conformer	congregate	connective
conformity	congregated	connivance

49

connive	conservative	consorted
connoisseur	conservatory	conspicuous
connotation	conserve	conspicuously
connote	conserved	conspiracy
connubial	consider	conspirator
conquer	considerable	conspiratorial
conquered	considerate	conspire
conqueror	consideration	conspired
conquest	considers	constable
conquests	consign	constabulary
consanguinity	consigned	constancy
conscience	consignee	constant
conscientious	consignment	constantly
conscientiously	consignor	constellation
conscious	consist	consternation
consciously	consistency	constipation
consciousness	consistent	constituency
conscript	consistory	constituent
consecrate	consists	constitute
consecrated	consolation	constituted
consecration	console	constitution
consecutive	consoled	constitutional
consensus	consolidate	constitutionality
consent	consolidated	constitutionally
consented	consolidation	constrain
consequence	consolingly	constrained
consequent	consols	constraint
consequential	consonance	constrict
consequently	consonant	constriction
conservation	consonantal	construct
conservatism	consort	constructed

50

constructive	contemptible	continuous
construe	contemptuous	continuously
construed	contend	continuum
consul	contended	contort
consular	contender	contorted
consulate	content	contortion
consulates	contented	contortionist
consult	contention	contour
consultant	contentious	contraband
consultation	contentment	contrabass
consultative	contest	contract
consulted	contestant	contracted
consumable	contestation	contractile
consume	contests	contraction
consummate	context	contractor
consummation	contextual	contradict
consumption	contiguity	contradiction
consumptive	contiguous	contradictory
contact	continence	contradis-
contagion	continent	tinction
contagious	continental	contraindicate
contain	contingency	contralto
contained	contingent	contraption
container	continual	contrary
contaminate	continually	contrast
contamination	continuance	contrasts
contemplate	continuant	contravene
contemplation	continuation	contravention
contemporaneous	continue	contribute
contemporary	continued	contribution
contempt	continuity	contributor
		contributory

51

contrite	conventionality	convocation
contritely	conventionalize	convoke
contrition	conventionally	convoked
contrivance	conventual	convolution
contrive	converge	convoy
control	convergence	convoyed
controllable	convergent	convulse
controlled	conversant	convulsion
controller	conversation	convulsive
controversial	conversational	cooker
controversy	conversationalist	cookery
controvert	converse	cool
contumacious	conversion	cooled
contumacy	convert	cooler
contumely	converted	coolest
contuse	convertibility	coolie
contusion	convertible	coolly
conundrum	convex	coolness
convalesce	convexity	coop
convalescence	convey	cooper
convalescent	conveyance	cooperage
convection	conveyed	co-operate
convene	conveyor	co-operation
convened	convict	co-operative
convenience	convicted	co-opt
conveniences	conviction	co-ordinate
convenient	convince	co-ordination
conveniently	convincingly	copartner
convent	convivial	copartnership
convention	conviviality	Copernican
conventional	convivially	copious

52

copiously	cornered	corresponds
copiousness	cornice	corridor
copper	cornucopia	corroborate
copperhead	corona	corroboration
copperplate	coroner	corroborative
coppersmith	coronet	corroboratory
copra	corporal	corrode
copy	corporate	corroded
copyright	corporately	corrosion
coracle	corporation	corrosive
coral	corporeal	corrugate
cord	corps	corrugation
cordage	corpse	corrupt
corded	corpulence	corrupted
cordial	corpulent	corruptible
cordiality	corpuscle	corruption
cordially	corpuscular	corruptly
cordite	corral	corsage
cordon	correct	corsair
Cordovan	correction	corset
corduroy	corrective	cortege
core	correctly	cortex
cored	correctness	cortical
corespondent	corrector	corundum
Corinthian	correlate	coruscate
cork	correlation	coruscation
corkscrew	correlative	coryza
cormorant	correspond	cosily
corn	correspondence	cosine
cornea	correspondent	cosiness
corner	correspondingly	cosmetic

53

cosmic	counterfeit	courthouse
cosmopolitan	counterfeiter	courtier
cosmos	counterirritant	courtliness
Cossack	countermand	courtly
cost	countermine	courtship
costliness	counterpart	courtyard
costly	counterplot	cousin
costume	counterpoint	cove
costumer	countershaft	covenant
coterie	countersign	cover
cottage	countersink	coverage
cotter	counterweight	coverlet
cotton	countess	coverlets
cottontail	countless	covert
couch	country	covet
cougar	county	covetous
cough	coupé	coward
could	couple	cowardice
council	coupler	cowardly
councilor	couplet	cowboy
counsel	couplets	cowcatcher
counseled	couplings	cowl
count	coupon	cowlick
counted	courage	coworker
countenance	courageous	coxcomb
counter	courier	coy
counteract	course	coyly
counterbalance	courser	coyness
countercharge	court	coyote
countercheck	courteous	crab
countered	courtesy	crack

54

cracker	crass	creator
crackle	crate	creature
crackled	crated	credence
cradle	crater	credential
cradled	cravat	credibility
craft	crave	credible
craftier	craven	credit
craftiest	cravenette	creditable
craftily	cravings	credited
craftiness	crawfish	creditor
craftsman	crawl	credo
crafty	crawled	credulity
crag	crayon	credulous
cram	craze	creed
crammed	crazier	creek
cramp	craziest	creep
cranberry	crazily	creeper
crane	craziness	creepiness
craned	crazy	cremate
cranial	creak	cremated
craniotomy	creakingly	cremation
cranium	cream	crematory
crank	creamery	Cremona
crankcase	creamier	creole
cranked	creamiest	creosote
crankily	creamy	crepitant
crankiness	crease	crepitate
cranky	create	crescendo
cranny	created	crescent
crape	creation	crest
crash	creative	crestfallen

55

cretin	criticize	crowbar
cretonne	criticized	crowd
crevasse	critique	crowded
crevice	croak	crown
crew	croaker	crowned
crewel	croakingly	crucial
crib	crochet	crucially
cribbage	crock	crucible
cricket	crockery	crucifixion
crime	crocodile	cruciform
criminal	crocus	crude
criminally	crook	crudity
criminology	crooked	cruel
crimp	croon	cruelly
crimson	crooned	cruelty
cringe	crooner	cruise
crinkle	crop	cruiser
crinoline	croquet	crumb
cripple	croquette	crumble
crises	crosier	crumpet
crisis	cross	crumple
crisp	crossbar	crumpled
crisply	crossbow	crunch
crispness	crosscut	crusade
crisscross	crossings	crusader
criteria	crossroad	cruse
criterion	crosswise	crush
critic	crotchet	crushingly
critical	crouch	crust
critically	croup	crusty
criticism	crow	crutch

crux	cull	curacy
cry	culled	curare
cryolite	culminate	curate
crypt	culminated	curative
cryptic	culmination	curator
cryptical	culpability	curb
cryptically	culpable	curbed
cryptogram	culprit	curd
cryptograph	cult	cure
cryptography	cultivate	cured
crystal	cultivated	curette
crystalline	cultivation	curfew
crystallization	cultivator	curio
crystallize	cultural	curiosities
crystallized	culturally	curiosity
cub	culture	curious
cube	cultured	curiously
cubeb	culvert	curl
cubic	cumbersome	curled
cubicle	cumulative	curler
cubit	cuneiform	curlicue
cuckoo	cunningly	curly
cucumber	cupboard	curmudgeon
cuddle	cupel	currant
cuddled	cupellation	currency
cudgel	cupful	current
cue	Cupid	currently
cuff	cupidity	curricula
cuirass	cupola	curriculum
cuisine	cur	curse
culinary	curable	cursive

57

cursory	cute	cyclopedic
curt	cuticle	Cyclops
curtail	cutlass	cyclotron
curtain	cutlery	cygnet
curtly	cutlet	cylinder
curvature	cutlets	cylindric
curve	cutout	cylindrical
curved	cutter	cymbal
cushion	cuttings	cynic
cusp	cuttlefish	cynical
cuspidor	cyanate	cynically
custard	cyanic	cynicism
custodial	cyanide	cynosure
custodian	cyanite	cypress
custody	cyanogen	cyst
custom	cyanosis	cystitis
customarily	cycle	cystoid
customary	cyclometer	cystolith
customer	cyclone	cystotomy
cut	cyclonic	czar
cutaneous	cyclopedia	Czech

D

dachshund
dacoit
daedal
daffodil
daft
dagger
daguerreotype
dahlia
daily
daintier
daintiest
daintily
daintiness
dainty
dairy
dairyman
dais
daisy
dalliance
dally
dalmatian
dam
damage
damaged
damascene
damascus
damask

dammed
damnable
damp
dampen
dampened
damper
dampest
dampness
dance
dancer
dandelion
dandle
dandled
dandruff
dandy
danger
dangerous
dangerously
dangle
dangled
Danish
dank
dapper
dapple
dappled
dare
dared

daringly
dark
darken
darker
darkest
darkly
darkness
darling
dart
dash
dastardly
data
date
dated
dative
datum
daub
daughter
daughter-in-law
daunt
daunted
dauntless
dauphin
davenport
davit
dawdle
dawdled

dawn	dearer	decade
dawned	dearest	decadence
day	dearly	decadent
daybook	dearth	decalcomania
daybreak	death	decant
daydream	deathbed	decanter
daylight	deathblow	decapitate
daytime	deathless	decapitation
dazzle	deathly	decathlon
dazzled	debacle	decay
dazzlingly	debar	decease
deacon	debark	decedent
dead	debarred	deceit
deaden	debase	deceitful
deadened	debased	deceive
deadfall	debasement	deceived
deadhead	debatable	deceleration
deadlock	debate	December
deadly	debated	decency
deaf	debater	decennial
deafen	debauch	decent
deafened	debauchery	decently
deafeningly	debenture	decentralization
deafer	debilitate	decentralize
deafest	debilitated	deception
deal	debility	deceptive
dealer	debit	deceptively
dealings	debited	decide
dean	debt	decidedly
deanery	debtor	deciduous
dear	debut	decimal

60

decimate	decoration	deepen
decimation	decorative	deepened
decipher	decorator	deeper
decipherable	decorous	deepest
deciphered	decorously	deeply
decision	decorum	deepness
decisive	decoy	deer
decisively	decrease	deerskin
decisiveness	decreased	deface
deck	decreasingly	defacement
deckle	decree	defalcate
declaim	decrepitude	defalcated
declamation	decretal	defalcation
declamatory	decried	defamation
declaration	decry	defamatory
declarative	dedicate	defame
declaratory	dedicated	defamed
declare	dedication	default
declared	dedicatory	defaulter
declension	deduce	defeasible
declination	deduced	defeat
decline	deducible	defect
declined	deduct	defection
declivity	deductible	defective
decoction	deduction	defend
decompose	deductively	defendant
decomposition	deed	defended
decontaminate	deeded	defender
decontamination	deem	defense
decorate	deemed	defensible
decorated	deep	defensive

61

defensively	deformation	delay
defer	deformed	delectable
deference	deformity	delectation
deferential	defraud	delegate
deferment	defrauded	delegated
deferred	defray	delegation
defiance	defrayed	delete
defiant	deft	deleted
defiantly	deftly	deleterious
deficiency	defunct	deletion
deficient	defy	delftware
deficit	degeneracy	deliberate
defilade	degenerate	deliberation
defile	degenerately	deliberative
defiled	degeneration	delicacy
defilement	degradation	delicate
define	degrade	delicately
defined	degraded	delicatessen
definite	degradingly	delicious
definitely	degree	deliciously
definiteness	dehydrate	delight
definition	dehydration	delightful
definitive	deification	delightfully
definitively	deify	delimit
deflate	deign	delimitation
deflated	deigned	delineate
deflect	deism	delineated
deflected	deist	delineation
deflection	deity	delineator
deforestation	dejectedly	delinquency
deform	dejection	delinquent

deliquesce	demobilize	denatured
deliquescence	demobilized	denial
deliquescent	democracy	denied
delirious	democrat	denizen
delirium	democratic	denominate
deliver	democratically	denominated
deliverance	democratize	denomination
deliverer	demolish	denominational
delivery	demolished	denotation
delphinium	demolition	denote
delta	demon	denoted
delude	demonetization	denounce
deluded	demonetize	dense
deluge	demonstrable	density
delusion	demonstrate	dent
delusive	demonstration	dental
de luxe	demonstrative	dentalgia
delve	demonstrator	dented
demagnetize	demoralization	dentifrice
demagogue	demoralize	dentist
demand	demoralized	dentistry
demandingly	demotic	dentition
demarcation	demountable	denunciation
demean	demur	denunciatory
demeanor	demure	deny
demented	demurely	deodorant
dementia	demurrage	deodorize
demerit	demurred	deodorized
demigod	demurrer	depart
demise	den	department
demobilization	denature	departmental

63

departure	depravation	dereliction
depend	deprave	deride
depended	depravity	derision
dependency	deprecate	derisive
dependent	deprecated	derivation
depict	deprecation	derivative
depiction	deprecatingly	derive
depilatory	deprecatory	dermal
deplete	depreciate	dermatitis
depleted	depreciated	dermatology
depletion	depreciation	derogatory
deplorable	depredation	derrick
deplore	depress	dervish
deplored	depressant	descend
deploy	depressingly	descendant
deployment	depression	descent
depolarization	depressive	describe
depolarize	deprivation	described
depopulate	deprive	description
deport	depth	descriptive
deportation	deputation	descry
deportment	depute	desecrate
depose	deputed	desecrated
deposed	deputize	desecration
deposit	deputy	desensitize
depositary	derail	desert
deposited	derailment	desertion
deposition	derange	deserve
depositor	deranged	deserved
depository	derangement	deservedly
depot	derelict	desiccant

desiccate	despoil	detained
desiccator	despoiled	detect
desiderata	despondency	detection
desideratum	despondent	detective
design	despot	detector
designate	despotic	detention
designated	despotism	deter
designation	desquamated	detergent
designed	desquamation	deteriorate
designer	dessert	deterioration
desirability	destination	determinable
desirable	destine	determination
desire	destined	determinative
desires	destiny	determine
desirous	destitute	determined
desist	destitution	deterred
desists	destroy	deterrent
desk	destroyer	detest
desolate	destructible	detestable
desolately	destruction	detestation
desolation	destructive	detests
despair	desuetude	dethrone
despaired	desultorily	detonate
despairingly	desultory	detonated
desperate	detach	detonation
desperately	detachable	detonator
desperation	detached	detour
despicable	detachment	detoured
despise	detail	detract
despised	detailed	detraction
despite	detain	detractor

65

detriment	devotional	diameter
detrimental	devour	diametric
detritus	devoured	diamond
devaluate	devoutly	diapason
devaluated	dew	diaper
devaluation	dewy	diaphanous
devastate	dexter	diaphanously
devastated	dexterity	diaphragm
devastation	dexterous	diastole
develop	dexterously	diastolic
development	dextrose	diathermic
developmental	diabetes	diatom
deviate	diabetic	diatonic
deviated	diabolic	diatribe
deviation	diabolical	dice
device	diaconal	dichotomy
devil	diacritical	dictaphone
deviltry	diadem	dictate
devious	diaeresis	dictated
deviously	diagnose	dictation
deviousness	diagnosed	dictator
devise	diagnoses	dictatorial
devised	diagnosis	dictatorially
devitalize	diagnostic	dictatorship
devoid	diagnostician	diction
devolve	diagonal	dictionary
devolved	diagram	dictograph
devote	dial	dictum
devoted	dialect	did
devotee	dialed	didactic
devotion	dialogue	die

died	dignity	dine
diet	digress	dined
dietary	digression	diner
dietetics	dike	dingily
differ	dilapidate	dingy
differed	dilapidation	dinner
difference	dilatation	dinosaur
different	dilate	dint
differential	dilation	diocese
differentiate	dilatory	diopter
differentiated	dilemma	diorama
differentiation	diligence	diphtheria
difficult	diligent	diphthong
difficulty	diligently	diploma
diffidence	dilute	diplomacy
diffident	diluted	diplomat
diffract	dilution	diplomatic
diffraction	dim	diplomatist
diffuse	dime	diplopia
diffused	dimension	dipper
diffusion	dimensional	dipsomania
dig	diminish	dipsomaniac
digest	diminuendo	direct
digestible	diminution	direction
digestion	diminutive	directive
digestive	dimity	directly
diggings	dimly	directness
digit	dimmed	director
digitalis	dimmer	directorate
dignify	dimmest	directory
dignitary	dimness	direful

direst	disarrange	discipline
dirge	disarray	disciplined
dirigible	disarticulate	disclaim
dirndl	disassociate	disclaimed
dirt	disaster	disclaimer
dirtily	disastrous	disclose
dirty	disastrously	disclosure
disability	disavow	discolor
disable	disavowal	discoloration
disabuse	disband	discomfit
disadvantage	disbanded	discomfiture
disadvantageous	disbar	discomfort
disaffected	disbarment	discommode
disaffection	disbarred	discompose
disaffirm	disbelieve	discomposure
disaffirmed	disbeliever	disconcert
disagree	disbelievingly	disconnect
disagreeable	disburse	disconnected
disagreement	disbursement	disconsolate
disallow	discard	disconsolately
disappear	discarded	discontent
disappearance	discern	discontented
disappoint	discerned	discontent-ment
disappointingly	discernible	discontinuance
disappointment	discerningly	discontinue
disapprobation	discernment	discontinued
disapproval	discharge	discord
disarm	discharged	discordant
disarmament	disciple	discount
disarmed	discipleship	discountenance
disarmingly	disciplinary	discourage

68

discouraged	diseased	dishonored
discouragement	disembarkation	disillusion
discouragingly	disembarrass	disinclination
discourse	disembody	disincline
discourteous	disenchant	disinclined
discourtesy	disengage	disinfect
discover	disesteem	disinfectant
discoverer	disfavor	disingenuous
discovery	disfeature	disinherit
discredit	disfigure	disintegrate
discreditable	disfigured	disinterested
discredited	disfigurement	disinterestedly
discreet	disgorge	disjoin
discrepancy	disgrace	disjoined
discrete	disgraced	disjoinings
discretion	disgraceful	disjunction
discretionary	disgruntle	disjunctive
discriminate	disguise	disk
discriminated	disguised	dislike
discrimination	disgust	dislocate
discriminative	disgustedly	dislocated
discriminatory	disgustingly	dislocation
discursive	dish	dislodge
discus	dishabille	disloyal
discuss	disharmony	disloyalty
discusses	dishearten	dismal
discussion	dishevel	dismally
disdain	dishonest	dismantle
disdained	dishonestly	dismantled
disdainful	dishonor	dismast
disease	dishonorable	dismasted

69

dismay	dispensation	disqualification
dismayed	dispense	disqualify
dismember	dispensed	disquiet
dismembered	dispersal	disquietude
dismemberment	disperse	disquisition
dismiss	dispersed	disregard
dismissal	dispersion	disrepair
dismount	dispirited	disreputable
dismounted	displace	disrepute
disobedience	displacement	disrespect
disobedient	display	disrespectful
disobey	displease	disrobe
disobeyed	displeasure	disroot
disoblige	disport	disrupt
disorder	disposal	disruption
disorderly	dispose	disruptive
disorganize	disposed	dissatisfaction
disown	disposition	dissatisfy
disparage	dispossess	dissect
disparagement	dispossessed	dissemble
disparagingly	disposure	disseminate
disparate	dispraise	disseminated
disparity	disproof	dissemination
dispassionate	disproportion	dissension
dispatch	disproportionate	dissent
dispatched	disputable	dissenter
dispatcher	disputant	dissentient
dispel	disputation	dissertation
dispelled	disputatious	disservice
dispensable	dispute	dissidence
dispensary	disputed	dissident

dissimilar	distilled	disturber
dissimilarity	distiller	disunion
dissimulate	distillery	disunite
dissimulated	distinct	disuse
dissimulation	distinction	ditto
dissipate	distinctive	ditty
dissipated	distinctively	diurnal
dissipation	distinctly	divagate
dissociate	distinctness	divan
dissociated	distinguish	dive
dissociation	distort	dived
dissolute	distorted	diver
dissolution	distortion	diverge
dissolve	distract	diverged
dissolved	distractingly	divergence
dissonance	distraction	divergent
dissonant	distrain	diverse
dissuade	distrained	diversification
dissuasion	distraught	diversify
distaff	distress	diversion
distal	distressingly	diversionary
distance	distribute	diversity
distant	distribution	divert
distaste	distributive	divest
distasteful	distributor	divide
distemper	district	divided
distend	distrust	dividend
distensible	distrustful	divider
distill	disturb	divination
distillate	disturbance	divine
distillation	disturbed	divined

71

divinely	dodged	domesticate
divinity	dodo	domesticated
divisibility	doe	domesticity
divisible	doeskin	domicile
division	doff	domiciliary
divisor	dog	dominance
divorce	dogcart	dominant
divorcee	doge	dominate
divorcement	dogged	dominated
divulge	doggerel	domination
divulged	dogma	domineer
dizzier	dogmatic	domineered
dizziest	dogmatism	domineeringly
dizzily	dogmatize	dominie
dizziness	dogtrot	dominion
dizzy	dogwood	domino
do	doily	donate
docile	doings	donated
docility	doldrums	donation
dock	dole	donative
docket	doled	donkey
doctor	doleful	donor
doctorate	doll	doom
doctrinaire	dollar	doomed
doctrinal	dolman	door
doctrine	dolphin	doorknob
document	dolt	doorsill
documentary	domain	doorway
documentation	dome	dope
dodder	domed	dormant
dodge	domestic	dormer

72

dormitory	dowager	dragon
dormouse	dowdier	dragoon
dorsal	dowdiest	dragooned
dory	dowdily	drain
dosage	dowdy	drainage
dose	dowel	drained
dot	doweled	drainer
dotage	down	drainpipe
dotard	downcast	drake
dote	downfall	dram
dotingly	downhearted	drama
dotted	downhill	dramatic
double	downpour	dramatics
doubly	downright	dramatist
doubt	downstairs	dramatization
doubted	downward	dramatize
doubter	downy	dramaturgy
doubtful	dowry	drape
doubtfully	doxology	draper
doubtingly	doze	drapery
doubtless	dozen	drastic
dough	drab	draw
doughboy	draft	drawback
doughnut	draftier	drawbar
doughty	draftiest	drawbridge
doughy	draftily	drawee
dour	drafty	drawer
dove	drag	drawings
dove	draggle	drawl
dovecote	draggled	drawn
dovetail	dragnet	drawplate

73

dray	dried	dropsy
drayage	drier	dross
drayman	driest	drought
dread	drift	drove
dreaded	driftwood	drown
dreadful	drill	drowned
dream	drilled	drownings
dreamed	drink	drowse
dreamier	drinkable	drowsily
dreamiest	drinker	drowsiness
dreamily	drip	drowsy
dreamless	drippings	drudge
dreamlike	drive	drudgery
dreamy	drivel	drug
drearily	driven	druggist
dreariness	driver	druid
dreary	driveway	drum
dredge	drizzle	drumhead
dredged	drizzled	drummed
dreg	droll	drunk
drench	drollery	drunkard
drenched	dromedary	drunken
dress	drone	dry
dressed	droningly	dryly
dresser	drool	dual
dressings	droolings	duality
dressmaker	droop	dubiety
dressy	drop	dubious
drew	dropper	ducal
dribble	droppings	ducat
dribbled	dropsical	duchess

74

duck	dully	dust
duckling	dumb	dusted
duckpin	dummy	duster
duckweed	dump	dustiness
duct	dumpling	dusty
ductile	dun	duteous
ductility	dunce	duties
dudgeon	dune	dutiful
due	dungaree	duty
duel	dungeon	dwarf
duelist	dunnage	dwarfish
duenna	dunned	dwell
duffer	dupe	dwellings
dug	duplex	dwelt
dugong	duplicate	dwindle
dugout	duplication	dwindled
duke	duplicator	dynamic
dukedom	duplicity	dynamism
dulcet	durability	dynamite
dulcimer	durable	dynamo
dull	durance	dynasty
dullard	duration	dynatron
duller	duress	dysfunction
dullest	during	dyspepsia
dullness	dusky	dyspeptic

E

each	eased	ecclesiastic
eager	easel	ecclesiastical
eagerly	easement	echelon
eagerness	easier	echo
eagle	easiest	éclair
eaglet	easily	éclat
ear	east	eclectic
earl	Easter	eclecticism
earldom	easterly	eclipse
earlier	eastern	eclogue
earliest	easterner	economic
early	eastward	economical
earmark	eastwardly	economically
earn	easy	economize
earned	eat	economized
earnest	eatable	economy
earnestly	eater	ecru
earring	eavesdrop	ecstasy
earshot	ebb	ecstatic
earthen	ebonize	ecstatically
earthenware	ebony	eczema
earthly	ebullience	eddy
earthquake	ebullient	edelweiss
earthward	ebullition	edge
earthwork	eccentric	edged
earthworm	eccentricity	edgeways
ease	ecchymosis	edgewise

edgings	effervescence	egress
edibility	effervescent	Egyptian
edible	effete	eider
edict	efficacious	either
edification	efficacy	ejaculate
edifice	efficiency	ejaculation
edify	efficient	eject
edit	effigies	ejection
edited	effigy	ejectment
edition	efflorescence	ejector
editor	efflorescent	elaborate
editorial	effluvia	elaborately
editorially	effluvium	elaboration
educable	effort	elapse
educate	effortless	elastic
education	effrontery	elasticity
educational	effulgence	elated
educationally	effulgent	elation
educator	effusion	elbow
eel	effusive	elbowed
efface	effusively	elbowroom
effacement	effusiveness	elder
effect	eggnog	elderberry
effected	eggplant	elderly
effective	eggshell	eldest
effectual	ego	elect
effectually	egoism	election
effectuate	egoist	electioneer
effeminacy	egotistic	elective
effeminate	egotistical	elector
effervesce	egregious	electoral

77

electorate
electrical
electrically
electrician
electricity
electrification
electrify
electrocute
electrocution
electrode
electrolier
electrolysis
electrolytic
electrolytical
electrolyze
electromagnet
electrometer
electron
electronic
electroplate
electropositive
electroscope
electrotype
eleemosynary
elegance
elegant
elegy
element
elemental
elementally
elementary

elephant
elephantiasis
elephantine
elevate
elevation
elevator
elfin
elicit
elide
eligibility
eligible
eliminate
eliminated
elimination
eliminative
elision
elite
elixir
Elizabethan
elk
ellipsis
ellipsoid
elliptic
elliptical
elm
elocution
elocutionist
elongate
elongated
elongation
elope

elopement
eloquence
eloquent
eloquently
else
elsewhere
elucidate
elucidated
elucidation
elude
eluded
elusive
emaciate
emaciated
emaciation
emanate
emanated
emanation
emancipate
emancipated
emancipation
emancipator
emasculate
emasculation
embalm
embalmer
embankment
embargo
embarkation
embarrass
embarrassed

embarrassment	embryo	emphatic
embassy	embryonic	empire
embattle	emend	empiric
embattled	emendation	empirical
embellish	emerald	empiricism
embellishment	emerge	emplacement
ember	emergence	employ
embezzle	emergency	employee
embezzled	emergent	employer
embezzlement	emeritus	employment
embezzler	emery	emporium
embitter	emetic	empower
embittered	emigrant	empowered
emblazon	emigrate	empress
emblem	emigration	emptied
emblematic	eminence	emptily
emblematical	eminent	emptiness
embodiment	emissary	empty
embody	emission	empyema
embolden	emit	emu
emboldened	emitted	emulate
embolism	emollient	emulated
embolus	emolument	emulates
emboss	emotion	emulation
embrace	emotional	emulative
embrasure	emotionally	emulatory
embrocation	emperor	emulous
embroider	emphases	emulsification
embroidered	emphasis	emulsify
embroidery	emphasize	emulsion
embroil	emphasized	enable

79

enact	encroach	endowment
enacted	encroachment	endue
enactment	encumber	endurable
enamel	encumbered	endurance
enameled	encumbrance	endure
enamored	encyclical	endured
encamp	encyclopedia	enduringly
encampment	encyclopedic	endways
encaustic	encysted	endwise
encephalic	end	enemy
encephalitis	endanger	energetic
enchant	endangered	energies
enchanted	endear	energize
enchantingly	endeared	energized
enchantment	endeavor	energy
encircle	endeavored	enervate
encircled	ended	enervation
encirclement	endemic	enfeeble
enclave	endings	enfilade
enclose	endive	enfold
enclosure	endless	enforce
encomia	endlessly	enforceable
encomium	endlong	enforcement
encompass	endocrine	enforcer
encore	endocrinology	enfranchise
encounter	endoderm	engage
encountered	endogenous	engaged
encourage	endorse	engagement
encouraged	endorsement	engagingly
encouragement	endow	engender
encouragingly	endowed	engendered

engine	enlightened	entangle
engineer	enlightenment	entanglement
English	enlist	enter
Englishman	enlisted	enteralgia
engorge	enlistment	enterectomy
engorgement	enliven	entered
engrain	enlivened	enteritis
engrained	enmesh	enterotomy
engrave	enmity	enterprise
engraved	ennoble	entertain
engraver	enormity	entertained
engross	enormous	entertainer
engrossed	enough	entertainingly
engrosser	enrage	entertainment
engulf	enrapture	enthrall
enhance	enraptured	enthrone
enhancement	enrich	enthusiasm
enharmonic	enrichment	enthusiast
enigma	enroll	enthusiastic
enigmatic	enrolled	enthusiastically
enigmatical	enrollment	entice
enjoin	enshrine	enticed
enjoined	ensign	enticement
enjoy	ensilage	enticingly
enjoyable	enslave	entire
enjoyment	enslavement	entirety
enlarge	ensue	entitle
enlarged	ensure	entitled
enlargement	entablature	entity
enlarger	entail	entomb
enlighten	entailed	entombed

entombment	envoys	epizootic
entomologist	envy	epoch
entomology	enzyme	equable
entrails	eon	equably
entrance	ephemeral	equal
entrancingly	epic	equaled
entrant	epicure	equality
entrap	epicurean	equalization
entreat	epidemic	equalize
entreaty	epidermal	equalized
entrust	epidermic	equalizer
entrusted	epidermis	equally
entry	epidermoid	equanimity
entryway	epiglottis	equate
entwine	epigram	equation
enucleate	epigraph	equator
enucleation	epilepsy	equatorial
enumerate	epileptic	equerry
enumeration	epileptoid	equestrian
enumerator	epilogue	equiangular
enunciate	episcopal	equidistance
enunciation	episcopalian	equidistant
enunciator	episode	equilateral
envelope	episodic	equilibrium
enviable	epistemology	equine
envious	epistle	equinoctial
environment	epitaph	equinox
environmental	epithalamium	equip
environs	epithet	equipage
envisage	epitome	equipment
envoy	epitomize	equipoise

equitable	erroneous	espousal
equitation	error	espouse
equity	eructation	esprit
equivalent	erudite	espy
equivocal	erudition	esquire
equivocate	erupt	essay
equivocation	eruption	essayist
era	eruptive	essence
eradicate	erysipelas	essential
eradication	escalade	essentially
erase	escalator	establish
erased	escapade	establishment
eraser	escape	estate
erasure	escapement	esteem
erect	escarpment	esteemed
erectile	escheat	ester
erection	eschew	esthetic
erectness	escort	estimable
erg	escorted	estimate
ergo	escritoire	estimated
ergot	escrow	estimation
ermine	escutcheon	estimator
erode	Eskimo	estivate
erosion	esophagus	estoppel
err	esoteric	estrange
errand	esparto	estranged
errata	especial	estrangement
erratic	especially	estron
erratically	Esperanto	estuary
erratum	espionage	esurient
erred	esplanade	etch

83

etcher	European	eventuality
etchings	Eustachian	eventually
eternal	eutectic	eventuate
eternally	evacuate	ever
eternity	evacuated	everglade
ethane	evacuation	evergreen
ether	evade	everlasting
ethereal	evaded	everlastingly
ethereally	evaluate	every
ethical	evaluation	everybody
ethically	evanescence	everyday
ethics	evanescent	everyone
ethnology	evangelical	everything
ethyl	evangelist	everywhere
etiquette	evaporate	evict
etymological	evaporation	evicted
etymology	evaporator	eviction
eucalyptus	evasion	evidence
Eucharist	evasive	evident
euchre	evasively	evidently
Euclid	evasiveness	evidential
eugenics	even	evil
eulogistic	evening	evilly
eulogize	evenings	evince
eulogy	evenly	eviscerate
euphemism	evenness	evocation
euphemistic	event	evocative
euphonious	eventful	evoke
euphony	eventfully	evolution
Eurasian	eventual	evolutionary
eureka	eventualities	evolutionist

evolve	excel	exclosure
ewe	excelled	exclude
ewer	excellence	excluded
exacerbate	excellency	exclusion
exacerbation	excellent	exclusive
exact	excelsior	excommunicate
exaction	except	excommunication
exactitude	exception	excoriate
exactly	exceptional	excoriated
exactness	exceptionally	excoriation
exaggerate	excerpt	excrescence
exaggerated	excess	excrete
exaggeration	excesses	excretion
exalt	excessive	excretory
exaltation	excessively	excruciate
exalted	exchange	excruciated
examinable	exchequer	excruciatingly
examination	excipient	excruciation
examine	excise	exculpate
examined	excision	exculpated
examiner	excitability	exculpation
example	excitable	exculpatory
exasperate	excitant	excursion
exasperatingly	excitation	excusable
exasperation	excite	excuse
excavate	excitedly	excused
excavation	excitement	excuses
excavator	exclaim	execrable
exceed	exclaimed	execrate
exceeded	exclamation	execration
exceedingly	exclamatory	executant

85

execute	exhibit	expand
executed	exhibited	expanded
execution	exhibition	expanse
executioner	exhibitor	expansion
executive	exhilarate	expansive
executor	exhilaration	expatiate
executrix	exhort	expatiated
exegeses	exhortation	expatriate
exegesis	exhorted	expatriation
exemplar	exhumation	expect
exemplary	exhume	expectancy
exemplification	exigency	expectant
exemplify	exigent	expectantly
exempt	exiguous	expectation
exempted	exile	expectorant
exemption	exist	expectorate
exequatur	existence	expectoration
exercise	existent	expediency
exercised	exists	expedient
exerciser	exit	expediently
exert	exodus	expeditate
exerted	exonerate	expedite
exertion	exoneration	expedited
exhalation	exorbitant	expedition
exhale	exorbitantly	expeditionary
exhaled	exorcise	expeditious
exhaust	exorcised	expeditiously
exhaustion	exorcism	expel
exhaustive	exordium	expelled
exhaustively	exoteric	expend
exhaustless	exotic	expended

expenditure	exploited	expropriate
expense	exploration	expropriation
expensively	exploratory	expulsion
experience	explore	expunge
experienced	explored	expunged
experiences	explorer	expurgate
experiment	exploringly	expurgated
experimental	explosion	expurgation
experimentally	explosive	exquisite
experimentation	exponent	extant
experimenter	exponential	extemporaneous
expert	export	extempore
expertly	exportable	extemporization
expertness	exportation	extemporize
expiate	expose	extend
expiation	exposed	extended
expiration	exposition	extensible
expire	expositor	extension
expired	expository	extensive
explain	expostulate	extent
explained	expostulated	extenuate
explanation	expostulation	extenuated
explanatory	exposure	extenuation
expletive	expound	exterior
explicable	express	exterminate
explicit	expressage	exterminated
explicitly	expression	extermination
explode	expressive	exterminator
exploded	expressively	external
exploit	expressly	externally
exploitation	expressman	extinct

87

extinction	extraordinary	exudation
extinguish	extravagance	exude
extirpate	extravagant	exult
extirpated	extravaganza	exultant
extirpation	extravasate	exultation
extol	extravasation	exulted
extort	extreme	exultingly
extorted	extremist	eye
extortion	extremity	eyeball
extortionate	extricate	eyebrow
extra	extricated	eyelash
extract	extrication	eyeless
extraction	extrinsic	eyelet
extractive	extrude	eyelid
extradite	extruded	eyepiece
extradited	extrusion	eyes
extradition	exuberance	eyeshot
extraneous	exuberant	eyesight
extraordinarily	exudate	eyespot

F

Fabian	factual	faith
fable	factually	faithful
fabric	facultative	faithfulness
fabricate	faculties	faithless
fabrication	faculty	faithlessly
fabulous	faddist	fake
façade	fade	faker
face	faded	falcon
facet	Fahrenheit	fall
facetious	fail	fallacious
facial	failed	fallaciously
facile	failings	fallacy
facilely	faille	fallen
facilitate	failure	fallibility
facilities	faint	fallible
facility	fainted	fallow
facings	fainthearted	false
facsimile	faintly	falsehood
fact	faintness	falsely
faction	fair	falseness
factional	fairer	falsetto
factious	fairest	falsification
factitious	fairly	falsifier
factitive	fairness	falsify
factor	fairway	falsity
factory	fairy	falter
factotum	fairyland	faltered

89

falteringly	far	fat
fame	farad	fatal
famed	farce	fatalism
familial	farcical	fatalist
familiar	farcy	fatalistic
familiarity	fare	fatality
familiarize	fared	fatally
familiarly	farewell	fate
families	farina	fateful
family	farinaceous	father
famine	farm	fatherhood
famish	farmed	father-in-law
famous	farmhouse	fatherland
famously	farmyard	fatherless
fan	faro	fatherly
fanatic	farsighted	fathom
fanatical	farther	fathomless
fanaticism	farthest	fatigue
fancied	farthing	fatness
fancier	fascinate	fatten
fanciest	fascinatingly	fatter
fanciful	fashion	fattest
fancy	fashionable	fatty
fanfare	fast	fatuity
fang	fasten	fatuous
fanged	fastened	faucet
fanlight	fastenings	fault
fanned	faster	faultily
fantasia	fastest	faultless
fantastic	fastidious	faultlessly
fantasy	fastness	faulty

faun	federalist	felicity
fauna	federalization	feline
favor	federalize	fellow
favorable	federalized	fellowship
favored	federate	felly
favorite	federated	felon
favoritism	federation	felonious
fawn	federative	felony
fawned	fedora	felt
fealty	fee	felucca
fear	feeble	female
feared	feebleness	feminine
fearful	feeblest	femininely
fearless	feebly	femininity
fearlessly	feed	feminist
fearsome	feedback	femoral
feasibility	feedings	femur
feasible	feel	fen
feast	feeler	fence
feat	feelingly	fencer
feather	feelings	fend
featherweight	feet	fender
feathery	feign	fenestrated
feature	feigned	fenestration
featured	feint	Fenian
febrile	feldspar	fennel
February	felicitate	feral
fecund	felicitated	ferment
fecundate	felicitation	fermentation
fecundity	felicitous	fermented
federal	felicitously	fern

ferocious	festoonery	fidget
ferociously	fetch	fiduciary
ferocity	fetid	fief
ferret	fetish	field
ferreted	fetishism	fielded
ferric	fetlock	fieldpiece
ferrochrome	fetter	fiend
ferrotype	fettered	fiendish
ferrule	fettle	fiendishly
ferry	feud	fierce
ferryboat	feudal	fierceness
fertile	feudalism	fiercer
fertility	feudatory	fiercest
fertilization	fever	fiery
fertilize	feverish	fife
fertilized	feverishly	fig
ferule	few	fight
fervent	fez	figuration
fervently	fiasco	figurative
fervid	fiat	figuratively
fervidly	fib	figure
fervor	fiber	figured
fescue	fibroid	figurehead
festal	fibula	figurine
fester	fickle	filament
festered	fiction	filariasis
festival	fictional	filature
festive	fictitious	filbert
festivity	fiddle	file
festoon	fiddler	filed
festooned	fidelity	filial

92

filibuster	findings	fireside
filigree	fine	fireworks
filings	fined	firkin
fill	finely	firm
filled	fineness	firmament
filler	finer	firmer
fillet	finery	firmest
film	finespun	firmly
filmed	finesse	firmness
filmy	finest	first
filter	finger	firstly
filtered	fingered	firth
filth	fingerling	fiscal
filthier	fingerprint	fish
filthiest	finial	fisherman
filthiness	finis	fishery
filthy	finish	fishhook
filtrate	finished	fishline
filtration	finisher	fishwife
fin	finite	fishy
final	fiord	fissile
finalist	fir	fission
finality	fire	fissionable
finally	firearm	fissure
finance	firebrand	fist
financial	firebrick	fistic
financially	fired	fisticuffs
financier	firefly	fistula
finch	fireman	fit
find	fireplace	fitful
finder	fireproof	fitfully

fitness	flagstaff	flask
fitter	flagstone	flat
fittingly	flail	flatboat
fittings	flailed	flatfish
fix	flair	flatiron
fixation	flake	flatly
fixative	flakiness	flatness
fixed	flaky	flatten
fixings	flambeau	flatter
fixity	flamboyant	flattered
fixture	flame	flatterer
fizzle	flamed	flatteringly
fizzled	flamingly	flattery
flabbier	flamingo	flattest
flabbiest	flange	flatulence
flabbiness	flanged	flatulent
flabby	flank	flatware
flaccid	flanked	flatwise
flag	flannel	flatworm
flagellant	flannelette	flaunt
flagellate	flap	flaunted
flagellation	flapjack	flauntingly
flageolet	flare	flautist
flageolets	flared	flavor
flagitious	flash	flavored
flagon	flashboard	flavorings
flagpole	flasher	flaw
flagrance	flashily	flax
flagrant	flashiness	flaxen
flagrantly	flashingly	flay
flagship	flashy	flea

fleabite	flimsiness	floodlight
fleck	flimsy	floor
fledge	flinch	floppiness
fledgling	flinchingly	floppy
flee	fling	floral
fleece	flint	Florentine
fleeced	flintiness	floriculture
fleeciness	flintlock	florid
fleecy	flinty	floridly
fleet	flippancy	florin
fleetingly	flippant	florist
Flemish	flippantly	floss
flesh	flipper	flossy
fleshings	flirt	flotation
fleshy	flirtation	flotilla
Fletcherism	flirtatious	flotsam
flew	flirted	flounce
flex	flit	flounder
flexibility	flitch	floundered
flexible	flivver	flounderingly
flexure	float	flour
flick	floated	flourish
flicker	floater	flourishingly
flickeringly	flocculence	floury
flier	flocculent	flout
flight	flock	flouted
flightiness	floe	flow
flighty	flog	flower
flimsier	floggings	flowered
flimsiest	flood	floweriness
flimsily	flooded	flowerpot

95

flowery	flutings	foible
flowingly	flutist	foil
flown	flutter	foiled
fluctuate	fluttered	foist
fluctuated	flutteringly	fold
fluctuation	fluttery	folded
flue	flux	folder
fluency	fluxion	foliage
fluent	fly	foliate
fluently	flyer	foliation
fluff	flyleaf	folio
fluffiness	flytrap	folk
fluffy	flywheel	folkway
fluid	foal	follicle
fluidity	foaled	follicular
fluidly	foam	follow
fluke	foamed	followed
flume	foamier	follower
flung	foamiest	folly
flunk	foaminess	foment
flunked	foamy	fomentation
flunky	fob	fomented
fluorescence	focal	fond
fluorescent	focalize	fondant
fluorine	focus	fonder
fluoroscope	fodder	fondest
flurry	foe	fondle
flush	foeman	fondled
fluster	fog	fondly
flustered	foggy	fondness
fluted	foghorn	fondue

font	footstep	foreclosed
food	footstool	foreclosure
fool	footwear	foredeck
fooled	foozle	foredoom
foolhardy	foozled	foredoomed
foolish	foppery	forefather
foolishly	for	forefinger
foolishness	forage	forefoot
foolproof	forasmuch	forefront
foolscap	foray	foregone
foot	forbear	foreground
footage	forbearance	forehanded
football	forbid	forehead
footboard	forbidden	foreign
footbridge	forbiddingly	foreigner
footed	forebore	foreknowledge
footfall	force	foreleg
footgear	forceful	forelock
foothill	forcemeat	foreman
foothold	forceps	foremast
footings	forces	foremost
footless	forcible	forename
footlights	ford	forenoon
footman	forded	forensic
footmark	forearm	foreordain
footnote	forebear	foreordained
footpace	forebode	forequarter
footpad	forebodings	forerunner
footpath	forecast	foresee
footprint	forecastle	foreshadow
footrest	foreclose	foreshore

97

foresight	forgo	forsythia
forest	forgot	fort
forestall	forgotten	fortalice
forestalled	fork	forth
forestation	forked	forthcoming
forested	forlorn	forthright
forester	form	forthrightness
forestry	formal	forthwith
forests	formaldehyde	fortification
foretaste	formalism	fortify
foretell	formality	fortitude
forethought	formalize	fortnight
foretold	formally	fortnightly
forever	format	fortress
forewoman	formation	fortuitous
foreword	formative	fortunate
forfeit	formed	fortune
forfeiture	former	forum
forgather	formerly	forward
forgave	formic	forwarded
forge	formidable	forwarder
forgery	formula	forwardness
forget	formulate	fossil
forgetful	formulated	fossiliferous
forgetfully	formulates	fossilization
forgetfulness	formulation	fossilize
forgivable	forsake	fossilized
forgive	forsaken	foster
forgiven	forsook	fostered
forgiveness	forsooth	fought
forgivingly	forswear	foul

foulard	fragility	frazzled
fouler	fragment	freak
foulest	fragmentary	freakish
foully	fragmentation	freckle
foulness	fragrance	freckled
found	fragrant	free
foundation	fragrantly	freeboard
founded	frail	freeborn
founder	frailty	freedom
foundling	frame	freehand
foundry	framed	freely
fount	framework	freeman
fountain	franc	Freemason
fountainhead	franchise	Freemasonry
foursome	frank	freestone
fowl	frankfurter	freeze
fox	frankly	freezer
foxglove	frankness	freight
foxier	frantic	freighter
foxiest	fraternal	French
foxy	fraternally	frenzied
fracas	fraternity	frenzy
fraction	fraternization	frequency
fractional	fraternize	frequent
fractionally	fraternized	frequently
fractionate	fratricide	fresco
fractionation	fraud	fresh
fracture	fraudulent	freshen
fractured	fraught	freshened
fragile	fray	freshly
fragilely	frazzle	freshman

fret	fringe	froth
fretful	frippery	frothed
fretwork	frisky	frothy
friability	fritter	froward
friable	frittered	frown
friar	frivolity	frowned
fricassee	frivolous	frowningly
friction	frivolously	frowzily
frictional	frizzle	frowzy
Friday	frizzled	froze
fried	frock	frozen
friend	frog	fructiferous
friendless	frogfish	frugal
friendlier	frolic	frugality
friendliest	from	frugally
friendliness	frond	fruit
friendly	fronded	fruiterer
friendship	front	fruitful
frieze	frontage	fruitfully
frigate	frontal	fruitfulness
fright	fronted	fruition
frighten	frontier	fruitless
frightened	frontispiece	fruitlessly
frighteningly	frost	fruitlessness
frightful	frostbite	fruity
frightfully	frosted	frump
frightfulness	frostfish	frustrate
frigid	frostily	frustration
frigidity	frostiness	fry
frigidly	frostwork	fryer
frill	frosty	fuchsia

fuddle	functionary	furnishings
fuddled	fund	furniture
fudge	fundamental	furor
fuel	fundamentally	furrier
fueled	funded	furriest
fugacious	funeral	furrow
fugitive	funereal	furrowed
fugue	funereally	furry
fulcrum	fungi	further
fulfill	fungible	furtherance
fulfillment	fungicide	furthermore
full	fungoid	furthermost
fuller	fungus	furthest
fullest	funicular	furtive
fully	funnel	furtively
fulminant	funnier	fury
fulminate	funniest	fuse
fulminated	funny	fused
fulmination	fur	fuselage
fulsome	furbelow	fuses
fumble	furbish	fusibility
fumblingly	furious	fusible
fume	furiously	fusilade
fumed	furl	fusion
fumigate	furled	fuss
fumigated	furlong	fussy
fumigation	furlough	futile
fumigator	furloughed	futilely
fun	furnace	futility
function	furnish	future
functional	furnished	futurity

G

gabardine
gable
gadfly
gadolinium
gadroon
gaff
gag
gage
gaiety
gaily
gain
gained
gainer
gainful
gainfully
gainsay
gaiter
galantine
galaxy
gale
galena
gall
gallant
gallantry
gallery
galley
gallium

gallon
gallop
gallows
gallstone
galvanism
galvanization
galvanize
galvanized
gambit
gambler
gamboge
gambol
gambrel
game
gameness
gammon
gamut
gander
gang
ganglia
ganglion
gangplank
gangrene
gangrenous
gangster
gangway
gap

garage
garb
garbage
garble
garden
gardener
gardenia
garish
garland
garlic
garment
garner
garnet
garnish
garnishee
garnisher
garnishment
garniture
garret
garrison
garrulity
garrulous
garter
gas
gaseous
gash
gasket

gasoline	gear	genetics
gasp	geared	genial
gastralgia	geisha	geniality
gastric	gelatin	genially
gastritis	gelatinize	genii
gastronomic	gelatinoid	genitive
gate	gelatinous	genius
gatehouse	gem	geniuses
gatekeeper	gemmed	genteel
gatepost	gender	gentian
gateway	genealogical	gentile
gather	genealogist	gentility
gatherer	genealogy	gentle
gatherings	genera	gentleman
gaucherie	general	gentlemen
gaudy	generalissimo	gentleness
gauge	generality	gentler
gauntlet	generalization	gentlest
gauntlets	generalize	gently
gauze	generalized	gentry
gave	generally	genuflect
gavel	generalship	genuflection
gavotte	generate	genuine
gay	generation	genuinely
gayety	generative	genuineness
gayly	generator	genus
gayness	generic	geodetic
gaze	generosity	geography
gazelle	generous	geological
gazette	generously	geology
gazetteer	genesis	geometric

103

geometry	giant	girded
geranium	gibber	girder
gerent	gibbered	girdle
germ	gibberish	girdled
German	gibbon	girl
germane	gibe	girlhood
germicide	giblets	girlish
germinal	giddiness	girth
germinant	giddy	give
germinate	gift	given
germinated	gifted	giver
germination	gig	gizzard
germinative	gigantic	glacial
gerund	giggle	glad
gerundial	giggled	gladden
gerundive	gild	gladdened
gesso	gilded	glade
Gestalt	gilder	gladiator
gesticulate	gill	gladiatorial
gesture	gill	gladiolus
gestured	gilt	gladly
get	gimbals	gladness
geyser	gimlet	Gladstone
ghastliness	gimlets	glamorous
ghastly	gin	glamour
gherkin	ginger	glance
ghetto	gingerly	glanced
ghost	gingham	gland
ghostliness	gingivitis	glandered
ghostly	giraffe	glanders
ghoul	gird	glandular

glare	glittered	glued
glared	global	glum
glaringly	globe	glut
glass	globular	glutted
glassful	globule	glutton
glasshouse	gloom	gluttonous
glassiness	gloomily	gluttonously
glassware	gloominess	gluttony
glassy	gloria	glycerin
glaze	glorification	gnarl
glazed	glorify	gnarled
glazier	glorious	gnash
gleam	glory	gnat
gleamed	gloss	gnathic
glean	glossal	gnaw
gleaner	glossary	gnawed
gleeful	glossily	gneiss
glib	glossiness	gnome
glibly	glossitis	gnomic
glide	glossy	gnomon
glided	glottis	gnu
glider	glove	go
glidingly	glover	goal
glimmer	glow	goat
glimpse	glower	goatfish
glint	glowered	goatherd
glioma	glowingly	gobble
glissando	glowworm	goblet
glisten	glucinum	goblets
glistened	glucose	goblin
glitter	glue	gocart

god	goodly	governmental
godchild	good-natured	governor
goddess	goodness	gown
godfather	goose	grab
godhead	gooseberry	grace
godhood	gopher	graceful
godless	Gordian	graceless
godlike	gore	gracious
godliness	gored	graciously
godly	gorge	grackle
godparent	gorgeous	gradation
godsend	gorget	grade
godson	gorilla	graded
goggle	gospel	gradient
goings	gossamer	gradual
goiter	gossip	gradually
gold	got	graduate
golden	Gothic	graduated
goldenrod	gotten	graduation
goldfinch	gouache	graft
goldfish	gouge	grafted
goldsmith	gouged	grafter
golf	goulash	grail
golfer	gourd	grain
gondola	gourmet	grained
gondolier	gout	grammar
gone	govern	grammarian
gong	governable	grammatical
goober	governance	granary
good	governess	grand
good-by	government	grandchild

grandee	grasp	graybeard
grandeur	graspingly	grayish
grandfather	grass	grayness
grandiloquence	grasshopper	graze
grandiloquent	grassplot	grazier
grandiose	grate	grease
grandly	grated	greasewood
grandmother	grateful	greasier
grandness	grater	greasiest
grandparent	gratification	greasily
grandsire	gratify	greasiness
grandson	gratingly	great
grange	gratis	greatly
granite	gratitude	greatness
graniverous	gratuitous	greed
grant	gratuity	greedier
granted	gravamen	greediest
granular	grave	greedily
granulate	gravel	greediness
granulated	gravely	greedy
granulation	graven	Greek
granule	graver	green
grape	gravest	greenback
grapeshot	gravestone	greener
graph	gravitate	greenery
graphic	gravitated	greenest
graphical	gravitation	greenhorn
graphics	gravitational	greenhouse
graphite	gravity	greenish
grapnel	gravy	greenness
grapple	gray	greenroom

107

greenwood	grindstone	grossly
greet	grinned	grossness
greeted	grip	grotesque
greetings	gripe	grotesquely
gregarious	gripper	grotto
gregariously	grisly	grouch
Gregorian	grist	grouchily
grenade	gristle	grouchy
grenadier	grit	ground
grenadine	grittiness	grounded
grew	gritty	groundless
grid	grizzle	groundling
griddle	grizzled	groundwork
gridiron	grizzly	group
grief	groan	groupings
grievance	groaned	grouse
grieve	groaningly	grout
grievous	grocer	grove
grievously	grocery	grovel
grill	grog	groveled
grilled	groin	grow
grim	grommet	grower
grimace	groom	growl
grime	groomed	growled
grimly	groove	grown
grimness	grope	growth
grimy	gropingly	grub
grin	grosgrain	grubbiness
grind	gross	grubby
grinder	grosser	grudge
grindingly	grossest	grudgingly

gruel	guidebook	gumption
gruesome	guided	gumshoe
gruff	guidepost	gumwood
gruffer	guidon	gun
gruffest	guild	gunboat
gruffly	guile	guncotton
grumble	guileful	gunfire
grumpiness	guileless	gunlock
grumpy	guillotine	gunman
grunt	guilt	gunner
grunted	guiltily	gunnery
guarantee	guiltless	gunny
guaranteed	guilty	gunpaper
guarantor	guinea	gunpowder
guaranty	guise	gunrunning
guard	guises	gunshop
guarded	guitar	gunshot
guardian	gulch	gunsmith
guardianship	gulden	gunstock
guardroom	gulf	gunwale
guardsman	gull	gurgle
guava	gullet	gush
gubernatorial	gullets	gusher
gudgeon	gullibility	gushingly
guerdon	gullible	gushy
guerrilla	gulp	gusset
guess	gum	gust
guesswork	gumbo	gustatory
guest	gumboil	gustily
guidance	gummosis	gusto
guide	gummy	gusty

gutter	guzzler	gyrate
gutteral	gymkhana	gyration
gutteralize	gymnasium	gyratory
gutterally	gymnast	gyrfalcon
gutteralness	gymnastic	gyro
guttersnipe	gynecologist	gyrocompass
guy	gynecology	gyroscope
guzzle	gypsum	gyrostat
guzzled	gypsy	gyves

H

haberdasher	hailstone	halter
haberdashery	hailstorm	haltingly
habiliment	hair	halyard
habit	hairbreadth	ham
habitable	hairbrush	hamlet
habitant	haircut	hamlets
habitat	hairpin	hammer
habitation	hairsplitter	hammered
habitual	hairspring	hammerless
habitually	hairy	hammock
habituate	halberd	hamper
habituated	halcyon	hampered
habitude	hale	hamster
hackle	half	hamstring
hackman	halfway	hand
hackneyed	halfwitted	handball
hacksaw	halibut	handbook
had	halitosis	handcuff
haddock	hall	handed
hafnium	hallow	handful
haft	Halloween	handicap
hag	hallucination	handicraft
haggard	hallucinatory	handier
haggle	hallucinosis	handiest
haggled	halo	handily
hail	halogen	handiness
hailed	halt	handiwork

111

handkerchief	harassment	harmonica
handle	harbinger	harmonious
handled	harbor	harmoniously
handmade	harbored	harmonization
handrail	hard	harmonize
handsome	harden	harmonized
handsomely	hardened	harmony
handspring	hardener	harness
handwriting	harder	harp
handy	hardest	harpist
hang	hardier	harpoon
hangar	hardiest	harpooned
hanged	hardihood	harpsichord
hanger	hardiness	harrier
hangman	hardly	harrow
hanker	hardness	harsh
hankered	hardship	harsher
hansom	hardware	harshest
haphazard	hardy	harshly
hapless	hare	harshness
happen	harebrained	harvest
happened	harelip	harvester
happenings	harem	has
happier	hark	hash
happiest	Harlequin	hashish
happily	harm	hasp
happiness	harmed	hassock
happy	harmful	haste
harangue	harmless	hasten
harangued	harmlessly	hastened
harass	harmonic	hastily

112

hastiness	hawker	headgear
hasty	hawkweed	headily
hat	hawse	headings
hatband	hawser	headland
hatch	hawthorn	headless
hatchery	hay	headlight
hatchet	haycock	headline
hatchment	hayfork	headlock
hatchway	hayloft	headlong
hate	haymow	headmaster
hated	hayrack	headpiece
hateful	hayseed	headquarters
hatefully	haystack	headsman
hatefulness	hazard	headspring
hatred	hazardous	headstone
hatter	hazardously	headstrong
haughtily	haze	headwater
haughty	hazel	headway
haul	hazily	headwork
haulage	haziness	heady
hauled	hazy	heal
haunch	he	healed
haunt	head	healer
haunted	headache	health
hauntingly	headband	healthful
have	headboard	healthfulness
haven	headcheese	healthier
haversack	headdress	healthiest
havoc	header	healthily
Hawaiian	headfirst	healthy
hawk	headforemost	heap

113

hear	heavenly	heinous
heard	heavenward	heir
hearer	heavier	heiress
hearings	heaviest	heirloom
hearken	heavily	helical
hearsay	heaviness	helicoid
hearse	heavy	helicopter
heart	Hebraic	heliotrope
heartache	Hebrew	helium
heartbeat	hecatomb	helix
heartbreak	heckle	helm
heartbroken	heckled	helmet
heartburn	hectic	helmeted
hearten	hectograph	helmsman
heartfelt	hedge	help
hearth	hedgehog	helper
hearthstone	hedgerow	helpful
heartier	hedonism	helpfully
heartiest	heed	helpfulness
heartily	heeded	helpings
heartless	heedfully	helpless
hearty	heedfulness	helplessly
heat	heedless	helplessness
heater	heedlessness	helpmate
heath	heel	hem
heathen	heft	hematite
heathenish	hegemony	hemicycle
heathenism	hegira	hemisphere
heather	heifer	hemlock
heave	height	hemorrhage
heaven	heighten	hemp

hemstitch	hereditable	herpes
hence	hereditament	herpetology
henceforth	hereditary	herring
henceforward	heredity	hers
henchman	hereinafter	herself
henequen	hereinbefore	hesitance
henhouse	hereon	hesitancy
hepatalgia	heresy	hesitant
hepatic	heretic	hesitate
hepatica	heretical	hesitated
hepatitis	hereto	hesitatingly
hepatotomy	heretofore	hesitation
heptagon	hereunto	heterodox
heptameter	hereupon	heterogeneity
heptangular	herewith	heterogeneous
herald	heritability	hew
heraldic	heritable	hewed
heraldry	heritably	hexagon
herb	heritage	hexagonal
herbaceous	hermetic	hexameter
herbage	hermetically	hexangular
herbal	hermit	hexapod
herbarium	hermitage	hiatus
herbivorous	hernia	hibernate
Herculean	herniotomy	hibernation
herd	hero	hibiscus
here	heroic	hickory
hereabouts	heroical	hid
hereafter	heroine	hidden
hereby	heroism	hide
hereditability	heron	hideous

115

hideously	hint	hoarser
hierarchy	hinted	hoarsest
hieratic	hinterland	hoax
high	hintingly	hobble
highborn	hippodrome	hobby
highboy	hippopotamus	hobnail
higher	hippopotamuses	hobnob
highest	hire	hobo
highland	hired	hock
highlander	hireling	hockey
highly	hirsute	hod
highness	his	hoe
highroad	hiss	hog
highway	histology	hogback
hike	historian	hogfish
hiker	historic	hoggish
hilarious	historical	hogshead
hilarity	history	hoist
hill	histrionic	hokum
hillier	hit	hold
hilliest	hitch	holder
hilliness	hither	holdings
hillock	hitherto	hole
hillside	hive	holiday
hilt	hoar	holily
him	hoard	holiness
himself	hoarded	holland
hinder	hoarder	hollow
hindered	hoardings	hollowed
hindrance	hoarfrost	hollowness
hinge	hoarse	holly

hollyhock	homunculus	hope
holocaust	hone	hopeful
holograph	honest	hopefully
holographic	honestly	hopefulness
holster	honesty	hopeless
holy	honey	hopelessly
holystone	honeybee	hopelessness
homage	honeycomb	hoplite
home	honeydew	hopper
homeless	honeyed	hopscotch
homelike	honeymoon	horde
homeliness	honeysuckle	horizon
homely	honk	horizontal
homeopathic	honor	horizontally
homeopathy	honorable	hormone
homesickness	honorably	horn
homespun	honorarium	hornbook
homestead	honorary	horned
homeward	honored	hornet
homework	hood	hornpipe
homicidal	hooded	horology
homicide	hoodlum	horoscope
homiletics	hoodoo	horrible
homilies	hoodwink	horrid
homily	hoof	horrification
hominy	hook	horrify
homogeneity	hooker	horror
homogeneous	hookup	horse
homogenize	hookworm	horseback
homologous	hoop	horsehair
homonym	Hoosier	horseman

117

horseshoe	hound	hug
horseweed	hounded	huge
horsewhip	hour	Huguenot
horsewoman	hourly	hulk
hortatory	house	hull
horticulture	housed	hulled
hose	housefly	hum
hosier	household	human
hosiery	householder	humane
hospice	housekeeper	humaneness
hospitable	housemaid	humanism
hospital	houseroom	humanitarian
hospitality	housetop	humanity
hospitalization	housewarming	humanization
hospitalize	housewife	humanize
host	housework	humanized
hostage	hovel	humankind
hostel	hover	humanly
hostess	how	humble
hostile	however	humbled
hostilely	howitzer	humbleness
hostility	howl	humbly
hot	howsoever	humbug
hotbed	hub	humdrum
hotel	hubbub	humerus
hotheaded	huckleberry	humid
hothouse	huckster	humidifier
hotly	huddle	humidify
hotness	huddled	humidity
hotter	hue	humidor
hottest	huff	humiliate

118

humiliated	hurtful	hydrometer
humiliation	hurtfully	hydrophobia
humility	hurtfulness	hydroplane
hummed	hurtle	hydroponics
hummock	hurtled	hydrostatics
humor	husband	hydroxide
humored	husbandry	hyena
humorist	hush	hygiene
humorous	hushed	hygienic
humorousness	husk	hygienically
hump	huskily	hymn
humus	huskiness	hymnal
hunch	husky	hyperactive
hundred	hussy	hyperalgia
hundredth	hustings	hyperbola
hunger	hustle	hyperbole
hungered	hustled	hypercritical
hungrily	hustler	hyperemia
hungry	hutch	hyperopia
hunk	hyacinth	hypertension
hunt	hyaloid	hyperthyroid
hunted	hybrid	hypertrophy
hunter	hydrangea	hyphen
huntsman	hydrant	hyphenate
hurdle	hydrate	hyphenated
hurdled	hydraulic	hypnosis
hurl	hydrocarbon	hypnotism
hurled	hydrochloric	hypnotist
hurricane	hydrocyanic	hypnotize
hurry	hydroelectric	hypochlorite
hurt	hydrogen	hypochondria

119

hypochondriac	hypotenuse	hypothetical
hypocrisy	hypothecate	hypothetically
hypocrite	hypotheses	hysteria
hypocritical	hypothesis	hysterical
hypodermic	hypothesize	hysterics
hypoglottis	hypothetic	hysteroid

I

iambic
Iberian
ibex
ibis
ice
iceberg
icebound
icehouse
iceman
ichneumon
ichor
ichthyology
icicle
icily
iciness
icy
icon
idea
ideal
idealism
idealist
idealistic
idealization
idealize
ideally
identical
identification

identify
identity
idiocy
idiom
idiomatic
idiosyncrasy
idiot
idiotic
idle
idled
idleness
idler
idly
idol
idolater
idolatrous
idolatry
idolize
idyl
idyllic
if
igloo
igneous
ignite
ignition
ignoble
ignominious

ignominy
ignoramus
ignorance
ignorant
ignorantly
ignore
iguana
ilex
Iliad
ilk
ill
illegal
illegality
illegibility
illegible
illegitimacy
illegitimate
illiberal
illicit
illimitable
illinium
illiteracy
illiterate
illness
illogical
illuminant
illuminate

121

illumination	immaculately	immorally
illuminator	immanent	immortal
illumine	immaterial	immortality
illusion	immature	immortalize
illusive	immaturely	immortally
illusory	immaturity	immovability
illustrate	immeasurable	immovable
illustrated	immediacy	immovableness
illustration	immediate	immovably
illustrative	immediately	immune
illustrator	immediateness	immunity
illustrious	immemorial	immunization
image	immense	immunize
imagery	immensely	immunology
imaginable	immensity	immure
imaginary	immerse	immutability
imagination	immersion	immutable
imaginative	immigrant	imp
imagine	immigration	impact
imaginings	imminence	impaction
imbecile	imminent	impair
imbecility	immobile	impaired
imbibe	immobility	impairment
imbroglio	immobilization	impale
imbue	immobilize	impaled
imitable	immoderate	impalement
imitate	immodest	impalpability
imitation	immolate	impalpable
imitative	immolation	impalpably
imitator	immoral	impanel
immaculate	immorality	impaneled

122

impart
imparted
impartial
impartiality
impartially
impassability
impasse
impassible
impassion
impassioned
impassive
impassively
impassivity
impatience
impatient
impeach
impeachable
impeachment
impeccability
impeccable
impeccant
impeccancy
impecuniosity
impecunious
impedance
impede
impediment
impedimenta
impel
impelled
impend

impenetrability
impenetrable
imperative
imperceptible
imperfect
imperfection
imperial
imperious
imperishable
impersonal
impersonate
impertinence
impertinent
imperturbable
impervious
impetigo
impetuosity
impetuous
impetuously
impetuousness
impetus
impiety
impinge
impingement
impious
impiously
impish
implacability
implacable
implant
implausible

implement
implicate
implication
implicit
implicitly
imploration
implore
imploringly
implied
imply
impolite
impolitely
impoliteness
impolitic
imponderable
import
importance
important
importation
importer
importunity
impose
imposingly
imposition
impossibility
impossible
impost
impostor
imposture
impotence
impotent

123

impound	improvable	inaccurate
impoverish	improve	inaction
impoverishment	improvement	inactive
impower	improvidence	inactivity
impracticability	improvident	inadequacy
impracticable	improvisation	inadequate
imprecate	improvise	inadmissibility
imprecation	imprudence	inadmissible
imprecatory	imprudently	inadvertence
impregnability	impudence	inadvertent
impregnable	impudent	inadvisability
impregnate	impudently	inadvisable
impregnation	impugn	inalienable
impresario	impugnable	inane
imprescriptible	impugned	inanimate
impress	impugnment	inanition
impression	impulse	inanity
impressionable	impulsion	inapplicable
impressionism	impulsive	inapposite
impressionistic	impunity	inappreciable
impressive	impure	inappreciative
imprimatur	impurely	inappropriate
imprint	impurity	inapt
imprison	imputable	inaptitude
imprisoned	imputation	inarticulate
imprisonment	imputative	inartistic
improbability	impute	inasmuch
improbably	inability	inattention
impromptu	inaccessibility	inattentive
improper	inaccessible	inaudibility
impropriety	inaccuracy	inaudible

inaudibly	inchworm	inclusively
inaugural	incidence	incognito
inaugurate	incident	incoherence
inauguration	incidental	incoherent
inauspicious	incidentally	incombustibility
inborn	incinerate	incombustible
inbred	incinerated	income
incalculable	incineration	incommensurable
incandesce	incinerator	incommensurate
incandescence	incipient	incomparable
incandescent	incise	incompatibility
incantation	incised	incompatible
incapable	incision	incompetence
incapacitate	incisive	incompetent
incapacitation	incisively	incomplete
incarcerate	incisiveness	incomprehensi-bility
incarceration	incisor	incomprehensible
incarnate	incitation	incompressi-bility
incarnation	incite	incompressible
incendiarism	incitement	inconceivability
incendiary	incivility	inconceivable
incense	inclemency	inconclusive
incentive	inclement	inconclusiveness
inception	inclination	incongruity
incertitude	incline	incongruous
incessant	inclined	inconsequential
incessantly	inclose	inconsiderable
incest	inclosure	inconsiderate
incestuous	include	inconsiderately
inch	included	inconsistency
inchoate	inclusive	inconsistent

125

inconsolable	incrustation	indefiniteness
inconspicuous	incubate	indelibility
inconstancy	incubation	indelible
inconstant	incubator	indelicacy
incontestable	incubus	indelicate
incontinence	inculcate	indelicately
incontinent	inculcation	indemnification
incontrovertible	inculpate	indemnify
inconvenience	inculpation	indemnity
inconvenient	inculpatory	indent
inconveniently	incumbency	indentation
inconvertibility	incumbent	indented
inconvertible	incunabula	indention
incorporate	incur	indenture
incorporation	incurable	independence
incorporator	incurably	independent
incorrect	incurred	indescribable
incorrigibility	incursion	indestructible
incorrigible	indebtedness	indeterminable
incorruptibility	indecency	indeterminate
incorruptible	indecent	index
increase	indecently	indexed
increasingly	indecision	indexer
incredibility	indecisive	indexes
incredible	indecorous	Indian
incredulity	indecorum	indicate
incredulous	indeed	indication
increment	indefatigable	indicative
incriminate	indefensible	indicator
incrimination	indefinable	indicatory
incriminatory	indefinite	indices

126

indicia	indistinct	inductive
indict	indistinctly	inductor
indictable	indistinguishable	indulge
indictment	indite	indulgence
indifference	indium	indulgent
indifferent	individual	indurate
indifferently	individualism	industrial
indigence	individualist	industrialism
indigenous	individualistic	industrialist
indigent	individuality	industrialization
indigestibility	individualize	industrialize
indigestible	individually	industrially
indignant	indivisibility	industrious
indignantly	indivisible	industriousness
indignation	indoctrinate	industry
indignity	indoctrination	inebriate
indigo	indolence	inebriation
indirect	indolent	inebriety
indirection	indomitable	inedible
indirectly	indoors	ineffable
indirectness	indorse	ineffably
indiscreet	indorsee	ineffective
indiscretion	indorsement	ineffectual
indiscriminate	indorser	ineffectually
indispensability	indubitable	inefficacious
indispensable	induce	inefficiency
indispose	inducement	inefficient
indisposed	induct	inefficiently
indisposition	inductance	inelastic
indisputable	inducted	inelasticity
indissoluble	induction	inelegance

inelegant	inexpedient	infelicity
ineligibility	inexpensive	infer
ineligible	inexperience	inference
ineluctable	inexperienced	inferential
inept	inexpert	inferior
ineptitude	inexplicable	inferiority
inequality	inexplicably	infernal
inequitable	inextricable	infernally
inequity	infallibility	inferno
ineradicable	infallible	inferred
ineradicably	infamous	infertile
inerrancy	infamy	infertility
inerrant	infancy	infest
inert	infant	infestation
inertia	infanticide	infidel
inertly	infantile	infidelity
inertness	infantilism	infield
inessential	infantry	infielder
inestimable	infarct	infiltrate
inestimably	infarction	infiltration
inevitability	infatuate	infinite
inevitable	infatuated	infinitesimal
inevitably	infatuation	infinitesimally
inexact	infeasible	infinitive
inexactitude	infect	infinitude
inexcusable	infected	infinity
inexhaustible	infection	infirm
inexhaustibly	infectious	infirmary
inexorable	infectiously	infirmity
inexpedience	infectiousness	inflame
inexpediency	infelicitous	inflamed

inflammability	infrequent	inhabitance
inflammable	infrequently	inhabitancy
inflammably	infringe	inhabitation
inflammation	infringed	inhabited
inflammatory	infringement	inhalation
inflate	infuriate	inhale
inflated	infuriated	inhaled
inflation	infuse	inhaler
inflationary	infused	inharmonious
inflect	infuses	inhere
inflection	infusion	inhered
inflexibility	ingenious	inherence
inflexible	ingeniously	inherent
inflict	ingenuity	inherently
infliction	ingenuous	inherit
influence	ingest	inheritable
influential	ingestion	inheritance
influenza	inglorious	inherited
influx	ingot	inheritor
inform	ingrain	inhibit
informal	ingrained	inhibited
informality	ingratiate	inhibition
informant	ingratiated	inhibitory
information	ingratiation	inhospitable
informative	ingratiatory	inhospitably
informed	ingratitude	inhuman
informer	ingredient	inhumane
informingly	ingress	inhumanity
infraction	ingrown	inimical
infrangible	inhabit	inimitable
infrared	inhabitable	inimitably

129

iniquitous	inkwell	inoculation
iniquitously	inky	inoffensive
iniquity	inlaid	inoperable
initial	inland	inoperative
initialed	inlay	inopportune
initially	inlet	inordinate
initiate	inlets	inorganic
initiated	inmate	inpatient
initiation	inmost	inquest
initiative	inn	inquietude
initiator	innate	inquire
initiatory	innately	inquired
inject	inner	inquirer
injected	innermost	inquires
injection	inning	inquiries
injector	innings	inquiringly
injudicious	innkeeper	inquiry
injudiciously	innocence	inquisition
injunction	innocent	inquisitive
injure	innocently	inquisitor
injured	innocuous	inquisitorial
injurious	innocuously	inroad
injury	innovate	insane
injustice	innovation	insanely
injustices	innovative	insanitary
ink	innovator	insanitation
inked	innuendo	insanity
inkhorn	innumerable	insatiability
inkling	inobservant	insatiable
inklings	inoculate	inscribe
inkstand	inoculated	inscriber

inscription	insignificant	inspiration
inscrutability	insincere	inspirational
inscrutable	insincerely	inspiratory
insect	insincerity	inspire
insecticide	insinuate	inspired
insectivorous	insinuated	inspirer
insecure	insinuatingly	inspiringly
insecurity	insinuation	inspiritingly
insensate	insipid	instability
insensibility	insipidity	install
insensible	insipidly	installation
insensitive	insist	installed
insensitiveness	insisted	installment
insentience	insistence	instance
insentient	insistent	instant
inseparable	insobriety	instantaneous
inseparably	insole	instanter
insert	insolence	instantly
inserted	insolent	instate
insertion	insolently	instead
inset	insolubility	instep
inshore	insoluble	instigate
inside	insolvable	instigated
insider	insolvency	instigation
insides	insolvent	instigator
insidious	insomnia	instill
insidiously	insomuch	instilled
insight	insouciance	instinct
insigne	inspect	instinctive
insignia	inspection	instinctively
insignificance	inspector	institute

131

instituted	insuppressible	intelligent
institution	insurability	intelligibility
institutional	insurable	intelligible
instruct	insurance	intemperance
instruction	insure	intemperate
instructional	insured	intemperately
instructive	insurer	intend
instructor	insurgency	intendant
instrument	insurgent	intended
instrumental	insurmountable	intense
instrumentalist	insurrection	intensification
instrumentality	insurrectionary	intensifier
instrumentally	insurrectionist	intensify
instrumentation	intact	intensity
insubordinate	intaglio	intensive
insubordination	intake	intent
insufferable	intangibility	intention
insufficiency	intangible	intentional
insufficient	integer	intentionally
insular	integral	intently
insularity	integrally	intentness
insulate	integrate	interact
insulated	integrated	interaction
insulation	integration	interborough
insulator	integrity	interbreed
insulin	integument	intercede
insult	intellect	interceded
insulted	intellectual	intercept
insultingly	intellectualize	intercepted
insuperable	intellectually	interception
insupportable	intelligence	interceptor

132

intercession	interleave	internally
intercessory	interline	international
interchange	interlineal	internationalize
interchangeability	interlinear	internationally
interchangeable	interlineation	interne
intercollegiate	interlined	internecine
intercommunicate	interlobar	internment
interconnect	interlock	interpellate
intercostal	interlocked	interpellation
intercourse	interlocutor	interplanetary
interdenominational	interlocutory	interpolate
interdependent	interloper	interpolated
interdependence	interlude	interpolation
interdict	intermarriage	interpose
interdiction	intermarry	interposition
interest	intermediary	interpret
interested	intermediate	interpretation
interestedly	interment	interpretative
interestingly	intermezzo	interpreted
interfere	interminable	interpreter
interfered	interminably	interregnum
interference	intermingle	interrelation
interferingly	intermingled	interrogate
interim	intermission	interrogation
interior	intermit	interrogative
interject	intermittence	interrogatory
interjection	intermittent	interrupt
interlace	intermittently	interruptedly
interlaced	intermixture	interruption
interlard	intern	interscapular
interleaf	internal	interscholastic

133

intersect	intolerable	introductory
intersperse	intolerance	introit
interstate	intolerant	introspect
interstellar	intonation	introspection
interstice	intone	introspective
interstices	intoned	introversion
interstitial	intoxicant	introvert
interstitially	intoxicate	intrude
intertwine	intoxicated	intruded
interval	intoxication	intruder
intervene	intractability	intrusion
intervened	intractable	intrusive
intervention	intramural	intrusively
interview	intransigence	intuition
interviewed	intransigent	intuitive
interviewer	intransitive	intuitively
interweave	intrastate	inunction
interwoven	intrenchment	inundate
intestacy	intrepid	inundated
intestate	intrepidity	inundation
intestinal	intrepidly	inure
intestine	intricacies	invade
intimacy	intricacy	invaded
intimate	intricate	invalid
intimated	intricately	invalidate
intimately	intrigue	invalidated
intimation	intrigued	invalidation
intimidate	intrinsic	invalidity
intimidated	introduce	invaluable
intimidation	introduced	invar
into	introduction	invariability

134

invariable	invidious	inwardness
invariableness	invidiously	iodate
invasion	invigorate	iodic
invective	invigorated	iodide
inveigh	invigoration	iodine
inveigle	invincibility	iodize
inveigled	invincible	ion
invent	inviolability	Ionic
invention	inviolable	ionization
inventive	inviolate	ionize
inventively	invisibility	iota
inventiveness	invisible	ipecac
inventor	invitation	Iranian
inventory	invite	irascibility
inverse	invited	irascible
inversion	invitingly	irate
invert	invocation	irately
inverted	invoice	iridectomy
invertible	invoices	iridescence
invest	invoke	iridescent
invested	invoked	iridium
investigate	involuntarily	iris
investigated	involuntary	Irish
investigation	involute	Irishman
investigative	involution	iritis
investigator	involve	irk
investiture	involved	irksome
investment	invulnerability	iron
investor	invulnerable	ironclad
invests	inward	ironed
inveterate	inwardly	ironical

135

ironside	irresolute	isolation
ironware	irresolution	isolationist
ironwood	irrespective	isomer
ironwork	irresponsibility	isomeric
irony	irresponsible	isotherm
Iroquois	irretraceable	issuance
irradiate	irretrievable	issue
irradiated	irreverence	issued
irradiation	irreverent	issues
irrational	irreversible	isthmus
irrationally	irrevocable	it
irreconcilability	irrigable	Italian
irreconcilable	irrigate	Italianate
irrecoverable	irrigated	italic
irredeemable	irrigation	italicize
irreducible	irritability	itch
irrefragable	irritable	itchier
irrefrangible	irritant	itchiest
irrefutable	irritate	itchy
irregular	irritated	item
irregularity	irritation	itemize
irrelevance	irritative	itemized
irrelevant	irruption	iterate
irreligious	ischium	itineracy
irremediable	isinglass	itinerancy
irremovable	Islam	itinerant
irreparable	island	itinerary
irreplaceable	islander	itinerate
irrepressible	isle	its
irreproachable	isobar	itself
irresistible	isolate	ivory

136

J

jabber	jarred	jersey
jabot	jasmine	jest
jack	jasper	jester
jackal	jaundice	jestingly
jackanapes	jaunt	Jesuit
jackdaw	jauntier	Jesus
jacket	jauntiest	jet
jackknife	jauntily	jetsam
jackstraw	jauntiness	jettison
Jacobean	jaunty	jetty
jade	javelin	jewel
jadeite	jawbone	jeweled
jaguar	jealous	jeweler
jail	jealousy	jewelry
jailed	jeer	Jewish
jailer	jeeringly	Jewry
jam	Jehovah	jibe
jamboree	jejune	jig
jammed	jellied	jigger
jangle	jelly	jiggle
janitor	jellyfish	jiggled
janitress	jeopardize	jigsaw
January	jeopardy	jingle
japan	jeremiad	jingled
Japanese	jerk	jingo
jar	jerkily	jingoism
jargon	jerky	jinrikisha

137

jinx	jolly	judicative
jitney	jonquil	judicatory
job	jostle	judicature
jobber	jostled	judicial
jockey	jot	judicially
jocose	jounce	judiciary
jocosely	journal	judicious
jocosity	journalism	juggle
jocular	journalist	juggled
jocularity	journalize	juggler
jocularly	journey	jugular
jocund	journeyed	juice
jocundity	jovial	juicy
jog	joviality	julep
jogged	jovially	July
joggle	jowl	jumble
join	joy	jumbo
joinder	joyful	jump
joined	joyfully	jumper
joiner	joyfulness	junction
joinings	joyless	juncture
joint	joyous	June
jointed	jubilance	jungle
jointly	jubilant	junior
jointure	jubilate	juniper
joist	jubilation	junk
joke	jubilee	junket
joker	judge	jurat
jokingly	judged	juridical
jollification	judgeship	jurisconsult
jollity	judgment	jurisdiction

jurisprudence	justice	justly
jurist	justifiable	justness
juror	justification	jute
jury	justificatory	juvenile
juryman	justified	juvenility
just	justify	juxtaposition

K

kaiser	ketosis	kinder
kale	kettle	kindest
kaleidoscope	key	kindle
kaleidoscopic	keyboard	kindled
kangaroo	keyed	kindliness
kaolin	khaki	kindly
kapok	khedive	kindness
karma	kibitzer	kindred
kava	kick	kine
kayak	kicker	kinesthetic
keel	kid	kinetic
keen	kidnap	king
keenly	kidnaped	kingbird
keenness	kidney	kingbolt
keep	kilerg	kingcraft
keeper	kill	kingdom
keg	killed	kingfish
kelp	killer	kingfisher
kennel	killings	kinglet
kept	kiln	kinglets
keratin	kilocycle	kingliness
kerchief	kilogram	kingly
kernel	kilometer	kingpin
kerosene	kilt	kingship
kersey	kilted	kink
kestrel	kin	kinship
ketch	kind	kinsman

kiosk	knifed	knowable
kipper	knight	knowingly
kitchen	knighted	knowingness
kitchenette	knighthood	knowledge
kite	knightliness	known
kith	knightly	knuckle
kitten	knights	knuckled
kleptomania	knit	knurl
kleptomaniac	knitter	knurled
klieg	knives	knurly
knapsack	knob	kobold
knave	knock	kodak
knavery	knockdown	kohlrabi
knavish	knocker	kopeck
kneecap	knockout	Koran
kneel	knoll	kosher
kneeled	knot	kraft
knelt	knothole	kremlin
knew	knotted	kulak
knickers	knotty	krypton
knickknack	knout	kymograph
knife	know	kyphosis

L

label	lactation	lamed
labeled	lacteal	lamely
labial	lactic	lameness
labor	lactose	lament
laboratory	lacuna	lamentable
labored	lacunae	lamentation
laborer	ladder	lamented
laborious	laden	lamina
laboriously	ladle	laminate
laburnum	ladled	laminated
labyrinth	lady	lamination
lace	ladylike	lampoon
laced	ladyship	lamprey
lacerate	lag	lance
lacerated	laggard	lancer
laceration	lagged	lancet
laches	lagoon	lancinating
lachrymal	lair	lancination
lachrymose	laird	land
lacings	laity	landau
lack	lake	landed
lackey	lambdoid	landfall
laconic	lambent	landholder
lacquer	lambkin	landlady
lacquered	lamblike	landlocked
lacrosse	lambrequin	landlord
lactate	lame	landmark

142

landscape	larger	lately
landslip	largess	latency
landsman	largest	lateness
landward	lariat	latent
language	lark	later
languid	larkspur	lateral
languish	larva	laterally
languishingly	larvae	latest
languor	larval	lath
languorous	laryngeal	lather
lanky	laryngitis	laths
lanolin	larynx	Latin
lansdowne	lascar	Latinism
lantern	lascivious	Latinity
lanthanum	lash	latitude
lanyard	lashed	latitudinal
lap	lashings	latitudinarian
lapel	lassitude	latter
lapful	lasso	lattermost
lapidary	last	lattice
lapse	lasted	latticework
lapsed	lastingly	laud
lapwing	lastly	laudability
larboard	lasts	laudable
larcenous	Latakia	laudanum
larceny	latch	laudation
larch	latched	laudatory
lard	latchkey	laugh
large	latchstring	laughable
largely	late	laughingly
largeness	lateen	laughingstock

143

laughter	layer	leased
launch	layman	leasehold
launchings	lazaretto	leaseholder
launder	lazier	leash
laundered	laziest	least
laundress	lazily	leather
laundry	laziness	leatheret
laundryman	lazy	leathern
laureate	leach	leatheroid
laurel	lead	leathery
lava	leaden	leave
lavalliere	leader	leaven
lavatory	leadership	leavings
lavender	leadsman	lecithin
lavish	leaf	lectern
law	leaflet	lecture
lawbreaker	leaflets	lectured
lawful	league	lecturer
lawfully	leagued	ledger
lawgiver	leak	leech
lawless	leakage	leek
lawlessness	leakiness	leer
lawmaker	leaky	leered
lawn	lean	leeringly
lawsuit	leaned	leeward
lawyer	leanings	leeway
lax	leap	left
laxative	learn	left-handed
laxity	learned	leg
laxly	learnt	legacy
laxness	lease	legal

legalism	leguminous	leper
legalistic	leisure	leprosy
legality	leisureliness	leprous
legalization	leisurely	lesion
legalize	lemon	less
legally	lemonade	lessee
legate	lemur	lessen
legatee	lend	lessened
legation	length	lesser
legato	lengthen	lesson
legend	lengthened	lest
legendary	lengthily	let
legerdemain	lengthiness	lethal
leggings	lengthways	lethargic
legibility	lengthwise	lethargical
legible	lengthy	lethargy
legion	lenience	lets
legionary	leniency	letter
legislate	lenient	lettered
legislation	leniently	letterhead
legislative	lenitive	letterpress
legislator	lenity	letters
legislature	lens	lettuce
legitimacy	Lent	leucocyte
legitimate	Lenten	leucocytosis
legitimately	lenticular	leucoderma
legitimateness	lentigo	leukemia
legitimation	lentil	levant
legitimatize	lentoid	levee
legitimist	leonine	level
legume	leopard	leveled

145

leveler	librarian	ligature
lever	library	ligatured
leverage	libretto	light
levitate	lice	lighted
levitation	license	lighten
levity	licensee	lightened
levulose	licentiate	lighter
levy	licentious	lighterage
lexicography	licentiousness	lightest
lexicon	lichen	lightheaded
liability	licit	lighthouse
liable	lick	lightly
liana	licorice	lightness
liar	lictor	lightning
libation	lie	lightship
libel	liege	lightweight
libeled	lien	ligneous
libelant	lieu	lignify
libelee	lieutenancy	lignite
libeler	lieutenant	likable
libelous	life	like
liberal	lifeguard	liked
liberalism	lifeless	likelihood
liberality	lifelike	likely
liberalization	lifelong	liken
liberalize	lifetime	likeness
liberally	lifework	likewise
liberate	lift	likings
liberation	ligament	lilac
liberator	ligate	liliaceous
liberty	ligation	lilt

146

liltingly	lineament	liquefy
lily	linear	liquescence
limb	lineman	liquescent
limber	linen	liquid
limbo	liner	liquidate
lime	linger	liquidated
limekiln	lingered	liquidation
limelight	lingerie	liquidator
limen	lingo	liquor
Limerick	lingual	lira
limestone	linguist	lisp
limewater	linguistic	lispingly
liminal	linguistically	lissome
limit	linguistics	list
limitable	liniment	listed
limitation	linings	listen
limited	link	listened
limitless	linkage	listener
limnology	linnet	listings
limousine	linoleum	listless
limp	linotype	litany
limpet	linseed	liter
limpid	lint	literacy
limpidity	lintel	literal
limpidly	lion	literalism
limply	lioness	literality
limpness	lionize	literalize
linden	lipoid	literally
line	lipoma	literary
lineage	liquefaction	literate
lineal	liquefiable	literature

147

litharge	livelong	localize
lithe	lively	locally
lithesome	liver	locate
lithia	livery	location
lithium	livid	loci
lithographer	livings	lock
lithographic	lizard	lockage
lithography	llama	locker
lithosis	llano	locket
lithotomy	load	lockjaw
Lithuania	loaded	lockout
litigable	loadings	locksmith
litigant	loaf	lockup
litigate	loafer	locomotion
litigation	loam	locomotive
litigious	loan	locus
litmus	loaned	locust
litter	loathe	locution
littered	loathed	lode
little	loathful	lodestar
littlest	loathly	lodge
littoral	loathsome	lodger
liturgical	loaves	lodgings
liturgy	lobar	lodgment
livable	lobby	loft
live	lobbyist	loftily
live	lobster	loftiness
lived	local	lofty
liveliest	localism	log
livelihood	locality	loganberry
liveliness	localization	logarithm

loggia	longitudinal	lose
logic	longshoreman	loses
logical	look	losings
logician	lookout	loss
logistics	loom	lost
logotype	loomed	lotion
logwood	loon	lottery
loin	loony	lotus
loiter	loop	loud
loitered	loophole	louder
loiterer	loose	loudest
loll	loosely	loudly
lolled	loosen	loudness
lollipop	loosened	lounge
lone	looseness	louse
loneliness	looser	lout
lonely	loosest	loutish
lonesome	loot	louver
lonesomely	lop	lovable
lonesomeness	lopsided	love
long	loquacious	loveless
longboat	loquaciously	loveliness
longed	loquacity	lovelorn
longer	lord	lovely
longest	lordliness	lover
longevity	lordly	lovesick
longhand	lordosis	lovingly
longhorn	lordship	low
longingly	lore	lowborn
longings	lorgnette	lowboy
longitude	losable	lowbred

lower	lug	lurk
lowermost	luggage	luscious
lowest	lugger	lush
lowland	lugubrious	lust
lowliness	lukewarm	luster
lowly	lull	lustful
lowness	lullaby	lustily
loyal	lulled	lustiness
loyalist	lumbago	lustrous
loyally	lumber	lustrously
loyalty	luminary	lustrum
lozenge	luminescent	lusty
lubricant	luminiferous	lute
lubricate	luminosity	luxuriance
lubrication	luminous	luxuriant
lubricator	lump	luxuriate
lucent	lumpy	luxurious
lucid	lunacy	luxury
lucidity	lunar	lyceum
lucidly	lunatic	lyddite
luck	lunch	lymph
luckily	luncheon	lymphatic
luckiness	lunette	lymphoid
luckless	lung	lynx
lucky	lunge	lyonnaise
lucrative	lurch	lyre
lucre	lurched	lyric
lucubration	lure	lyrical
ludicrous	lurid	lyricism

M

macabre	madness	magnificence
macadam	madrigal	magnificent
macadamize	maffia	magnifico
macaroni	magazine	magnifier
macaroon	magenta	magnify
macaw	maggot	magniloquent
macerate	Magi	magnitude
maceration	magic	magnolia
Mach	magical	magnum
machete	magician	magpie
machicolation	magisterial	maguey
machinate	magistracy	maharajah
machination	magistral	mahatma
machine	magistrate	mahogany
machined	magistrature	maid
machinery	magnanimous	maiden
machinist	magnate	maidenhair
mackerel	magnesia	maidenhood
macrocosm	magnesium	maidenly
macron	magnet	maidservant
maculate	magnetic	mail
madam	magnetically	mailability
madder	magnetism	mailable
maddest	magnetization	mailed
madhouse	magnetize	mailer
madly	magneto	mailings
madman	magnification	maim

151

maimed	malaria	malleolar
main	malarial	malleolus
mainland	malassimilation	mallet
mainly	Malay	malmsey
mainmast	malcontent	malnutrition
mainsail	male	malodorous
mainsheet	malediction	malposition
mainspring	maledictory	malpractice
mainstay	malefactor	malt
maintain	maleficence	Maltese
maintainable	maleficent	maltose
maintenance	malevolence	maltreat
majestic	malevolent	malversation
majesty	malfeasance	mammal
majolica	malformed	mammon
major	malice	mammoth
majored	malicious	man
majority	maliciously	manacle
majuscule	maliciousness	manage
make	malign	manageability
make-believe	malignancy	manageable
maker	malignant	manageably
makeshift	malignantly	management
makings	maligned	manager
malachite	malignity	managerial
maladjustment	malignly	managerially
maladminister	malinger	managership
maladroit	malingerer	manatee
malady	mallard	mandamus
malapert	malleability	mandarin
malapropos	malleable	mandate

mandated	manifold	mantis
mandatory	manifolder	mantle
mandible	manikin	manual
mandibular	manipulate	manually
mandolin	manipulated	manufactory
mandrake	manipulates	manufacture
mandrel	manipulation	manufactured
maneuver	manipulative	manufacturer
maneuvered	manipulator	manumission
manganate	manipulatory	manure
manganese	mankind	manuscript
manger	manlike	Manx
mangily	manliness	many
manginess	manly	map
mangle	manna	maple
mangled	manner	mapped
mango	mannered	mar
mangrove	mannerism	marabou
mangy	mannerly	maraschino
manhole	mannish	maraud
manhood	manometer	marauder
mania	manometric	marble
maniac	manor	March
maniacal	manorial	marcher
manicure	mansard	marchioness
manicurist	manservant	marconigram
manifest	mansion	mare
manifestation	manslaughter	margarine
manifestly	manteau	margin
manifesto	mantel	marginal
manifests	mantilla	marginalia

marginally	marred	mashed
margrave	marriage	masher
marigold	marriageable	mashie
marinate	married	mask
marinated	marrow	masked
marination	marrowbone	masker
marine	marrowfat	mason
mariner	marrowy	masonic
marionette	marry	masonry
Marist	Mars	masquerade
marital	marshal	mass
maritime	marshaled	massacre
marjoram	marshiness	massage
mark	marshmallow	massive
marked	marshy	mast
markedly	marsupial	master
marker	mart	mastered
market	marten	masterful
marketability	martial	masterfully
marketable	martially	masterfulness
markings	martinet	masterly
marksman	martyr	masterpiece
marl	martyrdom	mastership
marlin	marvel	masterwork
marmalade	marveled	mastery
marmoset	marvelous	masthead
marmot	mascara	mastic
maroon	mascot	masticate
marooned	masculine	mastication
marplot	masculinity	masticatory
marquisette	mash	mastiff

mastodon	matriculates	May
mastoid	matriculation	mayhem
mastoiditis	matrimonial	mayonnaise
mat	matrimonially	mayor
matador	matrimony	mayoralty
match	matrix	mazurka
matchless	matron	meadow
matchlessly	matronly	meager
matchmaker	matter	meal
matchwood	mattock	mealtime
material	mattress	mean
materialism	maturation	meander
materialist	mature	meaningless
materialistic	matured	meaningly
materiality	maturely	meanings
materialization	matureness	meanly
materialize	maturity	meanness
materialized	matutinal	meantime
materially	maudlin	meanwhile
maternal	maul	measles
maternally	mauled	measurable
maternity	mausoleum	measurably
mathematician	mauve	measure
mathematics	maverick	measured
matinee	mavis	measureless
matriarch	mawkish	measurement
matriarchy	maxillary	measurer
matrices	maxim	meat
matricide	maximal	meatus
matriculate	maximize	mechanic
matriculated	maximum	mechanical

155

mechanically	medieval	melodiously
mechanician	medievally	melodrama
mechanics	mediocre	melodramatic
mechanism	mediocrity	melody
mechanization	meditate	melon
mechanize	meditated	melt
medal	meditation	meltable
medalist	meditative	melted
medalists	medium	meltingly
medallion	mediums	member
meddle	medlar	membership
meddled	meek	membrane
meddler	meekly	membranous
meddlesome	meekness	memento
media	meerschaum	memoir
medial	meet	memorabilia
median	meetings	memorable
mediate	megacycle	memoranda
mediated	megaphone	memorandum
mediation	meiosis	memorandums
mediative	melancholia	memorial
mediator	melancholic	memorization
medical	melancholy	memorize
medically	melanosis	memory
medicament	meliorate	menace
medicate	melioration	menage
medication	mellifluous	menagerie
medicative	mellow	mend
medicinal	melodeon	mendacious
medicinally	melodic	mendacity
medicine	melodious	mended

156

mendicancy	interest	metalloid
mendicant	meretricious	metallurgic
menhaden	merge	metallurgical
menial	merger	metallurgy
menially	meridian	metamorphose
meningitis	meringue	metamorphosis
mensuration	merino	metaphor
mensurative	merit	metaphorical
mental	merited	metaphysical
mentality	meritorious	metaphysician
mentally	meritoriously	metaphysics
menthol	mermaid	metastasis
mention	merrily	metatarsus
mentioned	merriment	meteor
mentor	merry	meteoric
menu	merrymaking	meteorite
mephitic	mesa	meteoroid
mercantile	mescal	meteorology
mercenary	mesh	meter
mercerize	mesmerism	methane
merchandise	mesmerize	method
merchant	message	methodical
merchantman	messenger	methodist
merciful	Messiah	methodize
merciless	messmate	methodology
mercilessly	metabolic	methyl
mercurial	metabolism	meticulous
mercury	metacarpal	metonymy
mercy	metacarpus	metric
mere	metal	metrical
merely	metallic	metrology

157

metronome
metropolis
metropolitan
mettle
mettlesome
mezzanine
miasma
miasmal
miasmatic
mica
micaceous
microbe
microbiology
microcephalus
microcosm
microfilm
micrometer
micron
microorganism
microphone
microscope
microscopic
microtome
Midas
middle
middleman
middleweight
midge
midget
midiron
midland

midmost
midnight
midriff
midshipman
midst
midstream
midsummer
midway
midweek
midwife
midwinter
midyear
might
mightily
mightiness
mighty
migraine
migrate
migration
migratory
mikado
milch
mild
milder
mildest
mildew
mildly
mildness
mile
mileage
milepost

miler
milestone
miliary
militancy
militant
militarism
militarist
militaristic
military
militate
militated
militia
milk
milkings
milkman
milkweed
milky
mill
milled
millenary
millennial
millennium
miller
milline
milliner
millinery
million
millionaire
millionth
millpond
millstone

millwright	ministerially	misalliance
Miltonic	ministration	misanthrope
mime	ministry	misanthropic
mimeograph	mink	misanthropical
mimetic	minnow	misanthropist
mimic	minor	misanthropy
mimicry	minority	misapplication
mimosa	minster	misapply
minaret	minstrel	misapprehension
minatory	minstrelsy	misappropriate
mince	mint	misappropriation
mincingly	minuend	misarrange
mind	minus	misbegotten
minded	minuscule	misbehave
mindful	minute	misbehavior
mine	minute	miscalculate
miner	minuteness	miscall
mineral	minutia	miscarriage
mineralogy	minutiae	miscarry
mingle	minx	miscegenation
mingled	miracle	miscellanea
miniature	miraculous	miscellaneous
minim	mirage	miscellanist
minimal	mire	miscellany
minimization	mired	mischance
minimize	mirror	mischief
minimum	mirth	mischievous
minion	mirthful	miscible
minister	mirthfully	misconceive
ministered	mirthless	misconception
ministerial	misadventure	misconduct

159

misconstruction
misconstrue
miscount
miscreant
misdate
misdeal
misdeed
misdemeanor
misdirect
misdirection
misdoubt
miser
miserable
miserliness
miserly
misery
misfeasance
misfire
misfit
misformed
misfortune
misgivings
misgovern
misguide
mishap
misinform
misinformed
misinterpret
misinterpretation
misinterpreted
misjudge

misjudged
mislay
mislead
misleadingly
mislike
mismade
mismanage
mismate
misname
misnamed
misnomer
misplace
misprint
misprision
mispronounce
mispronunciation
misquotation
misquote
misread
misreadings
misremember
misrepresent
misrepresentation
misrule
miss
missile
mission
missionary
missive
misspell
misspelled

misspellings
misspent
misstate
misstatement
mistake
mistaken
mistakenly
misteach
mistiness
mistletoe
mistook
mistranslate
mistranslation
mistreat
mistreatment
mistress
mistrial
mistrust
mistrustful
misty
misunderstand
misunderstood
misuse
mite
miter
mitered
mitigable
mitigate
mitigation
mitosis
mitral

mitten	modern	moisture
mix	modernism	molar
mixed	modernist	molasses
mixer	modernity	mold
mixture	modernize	molded
mnemonic	modernized	moldy
moan	modest	mole
moaned	modestly	molecular
moat	modesty	molecule
mob	modicum	molehill
mobile	modification	molest
mobility	modified	molestation
mobilization	modifier	molests
mobilize	modify	mollification
mobilized	modish	mollify
moccasin	modishly	mollusk
Mocha	modishness	molt
mock	modulate	molten
mockery	modulated	molybdenum
mockingly	modulates	moment
modal	modulation	momentarily
modality	modulator	momentary
mode	module	momently
model	modulus	momentous
modeled	mohair	momentum
moderate	Mohammedan	monarch
moderated	moiety	monarchial
moderately	moist	monarchism
moderateness	moisten	monarchist
moderation	moistened	monarchistic
moderator	moistener	monarchy

161

monastery	monosyllabic	moorish
monastic	monosyllable	moose
monasticism	monotone	moot
Monday	monotonous	mop
monetary	monotony	moraine
monetization	monotype	moral
monetize	monoxide	morale
money	monsoon	moralist
moneyed	monster	moralistic
mongoose	monstrance	moralists
mongrel	monstrosity	morality
monitor	monstrous	moralization
monitored	month	moralize
monk	monthly	moralized
monkey	monument	morally
monocle	monumental	morass
monody	monumentally	moratorium
monogamous	mood	moray
monogamy	moodily	morbid
monogram	moodiness	morbidity
monograph	moody	morbidly
monolith	moon	mordant
monologue	moonbeam	more
monomania	moonfish	moreover
monoplane	moonlight	morgue
monopolism	moonshine	Mormon
monopolist	moonstone	morning
monopolistic	moonstruck	mornings
monopolization	moor	morocco
monopolize	moored	moron
monopoly	moorings	morose

morosely	mother-in-law	mourned
morphine	motherland	mourner
morphinism	motherless	mournful
morphology	motherliness	mouse
morris	motherly	mouser
morsel	mother-of-pearl	mousse
mortal	motif	mouth
mortality	motion	mouthed
mortally	motioned	mouthful
mortar	motionless	mouthpiece
mortgage	motivate	movability
mortgagee	motivation	movable
mortgagor	motive	move
mortification	motley	moved
mortify	motor	movement
mortise	motored	mover
mortmain	motorist	movie
mortuary	motorists	movingly
Moslem	motorman	mow
mosque	mottle	mow
mosquito	mottled	mower
moss	motto	much
mossback	mound	mucilage
mossiness	mount	mucilaginous
mossy	mountain	muck
most	mountaineer	mucoid
mostly	mountainous	mucosa
motet	mountebank	mucous
moth	mounted	mucus
mother	mountings	mud
motherhood	mourn	muddier

muddiest	multiple	murdered
muddily	multiplex	murderer
muddiness	multiplicand	murderous
muddle	multiplicate	muriatic
muddled	multiplication	murk
muddy	multiplicative	murkily
mudfish	multiplicity	murkiness
muff	multiplier	murky
muffin	multiply	murmur
muffle	multitude	murmured
muffled	multitudinous	murmurer
muffler	multivalent	murmurous
mufti	mumble	muscadine
mug	mumbled	muscatel
mugginess	mummer	muscle
muggy	mummery	muscular
mulatto	mummification	muscularity
mulberry	mummify	muscularly
mulch	mummy	musculature
mulct	mumps	muse
mulcted	munch	mused
mule	mundane	museum
muleteer	municipal	mush
mullion	municipality	mushroom
multifarious	municipally	mushy
multifold	munificence	music
multiform	munificent	musical
multiformity	muniment	musicale
multigraph	munition	musician
multilith	mural	musicianly
multimillionaire	murder	musk

musket	muteness	myeloid
musketeer	mutilate	myoma
musketry	mutilated	myopia
muskmelon	mutilation	myopic
muskrat	mutilator	myosis
muslin	mutineer	myotic
muss	mutinous	myotomy
mussed	mutiny	myriad
mussel	mutter	myrrh
mussy	muttered	myrtle
must	mutterings	myself
mustache	mutton	mysterious
mustang	mutual	mysteriously
mustard	mutuality	mystery
muster	mutually	mystic
mustered	muzzle	mystical
mustiness	muzzled	mysticism
musty	my	mystification
mutability	mycology	mystify
mutable	mycosis	myth
mutate	mydriasis	mythical
mutation	mydriatic	mythological
mutative	myectomy	mythology

N

nacelle	narcotism	nation
nacre	narcotize	national
nacreous	narrate	nationalism
nadir	narration	nationalistic
naiad	narrative	nationality
nail	narrator	nationalization
nailed	narrow	nationalize
nainsook	narrowed	nationally
naïve	narrower	native
naïvete	narrowest	nativity
naked	narrowly	natural
namable	narrowness	naturalism
name	narwhal	naturalist
named	nasal	naturalistic
nameless	nasality	naturalization
namelessly	nasalize	naturalize
namely	nasally	naturalized
namesake	nascent	naturally
nankeen	nastier	naturalness
napery	nastiest	nature
naphtha	nastily	naughtily
napkin	nastiness	naughtiness
napoleon	nasturtium	naughty
Napoleonic	nasty	nausea
narcissus	natal	nauseate
narcosis	natation	nauseated
narcotic	natatorium	nauseous

166

nautical	necessitous	neglectful
nautilus	necessity	negligence
naval	neck	negligent
navigable	neckband	negligible
navigate	neckcloth	negotiability
navigation	neckerchief	negotiable
navigator	necklace	negotiate
navy	necktie	negotiated
neap	neckwear	negotiation
Neapolitan	necrology	negotiator
near	necromancy	Negro
neared	necropolis	negrophile
nearer	necropsy	neighbor
nearest	necrosis	neighborhood
nearly	nectar	neighborly
nearness	nectarine	neither
nearsighted	need	nematode
neat	needed	Nemesis
neater	needful	neolithic
neatest	needfully	neon
neatly	needier	neophyte
neatness	neediest	neoplasm
nebula	neediness	nepenthe
nebular	needle	nephew
nebulosity	needled	nepotism
nebulous	needless	nephralgia
necessarily	needlework	nephrectomy
necessary	nefarious	nephritis
necessitate	negation	nerve
necessitated	negative	nerveless
necessities	neglect	nervous

167

nescience	newly	nightwear
nest	newness	nihilism
nestle	newspaper	nihilist
nestled	newsreel	nihilistic
nether	next	nimble
nettle	nibble	nimbus
nettled	niblick	nipper
network	nice	nipple
neural	nicely	nirvana
neuralgia	niceness	niter
neurasthenia	nicer	nitrate
neurasthenic	nicest	nitric
neurectomy	nicety	nitride
neuritis	niche	nitrification
neurosis	nickel	nitrify
neurotic	nickeliferous	nitrogen
neutral	nickelodeon	nitrogenous
neutrality	nickname	nitroglycerin
neutralization	nicotine	nitrous
neutralize	niece	no
neutralized	niggard	nobility
neutrally	niggardly	noble
never	night	nobleman
nevermore	nightcap	nobler
nevertheless	nightfall	noblest
new	nightgown	nobly
newcomer	nightingale	nobody
newel	nightly	nocturnal
newer	nightmare	nocturnally
newest	nightshirt	nocturne
newfangled	nighttime	node

nodule
noel
noise
noiseless
noisier
noisiest
noisily
noisiness
noisome
noisy
nomad
nomadic
nomenclature
nominal
nominally
nominate
nominated
nomination
nominative
nominee
nonacceptance
nonadmission
nonagenarian
nonagon
nonappearance
nonattendance
nonce
nonchalance
nonchalant
nonchalantly
noncombatant
noncommissioned
noncommittal
noncommunicant
noncompliance
nonconducting
nonconductor
nonconformist
nonconformity
nonconsecutive
noncontagious
noncorrosive
nondescript
none
nonentity
nonessential
nonexistence
nonexplosive
nonfeasance
nonfeasor
nonforfeiture
nonfulfillment
nonintervention
nonmetallic
nonnegotiable
nonpareil
nonparticipating
nonpartisan
nonpayment
nonplus
nonprofessional
nonresidence
nonresident
nonresistance
nonresistant
nonsense
nonsensical
nonsubscriber
nonsuit
nontechnical
nonunion
nook
noon
noonday
noontime
noose
nor
norm
normal
normality
normally
Norman
Norse
north
northeast
northeaster
northeasterly
northeastern
northeastward
northerly
northern
northerner
northernmost

169

northland	notoriety	nudged
northward	notoriously	nudity
northwest	notwithstanding	nugatory
northwesterly	nought	nugget
northwestern	noun	nuisance
Norwegian	nourish	null
nose	nourished	nullification
noseband	nourishingly	nullify
nosebleed	nourishment	nullity
nosegay	novaculite	numb
nostalgia	novel	number
nostril	novelette	numberless
nostrum	novelist	numbness
not	novelize	numeral
notability	novelty	numerate
notable	November	numeration
notarial	novice	numerator
notary	novitiate	numeric
notation	novocain	numerical
notch	now	numerous
note	nowadays	numismatics
notebook	nowhere	numismatist
noted	noxious	nunnery
noteworthy	noxiousness	nuptial
nothing	nozzle	nurse
nothingness	nuclear	nursemaid
notice	nucleate	nursery
noticeable	nucleation	nurseryman
notification	nucleus	nurture
notify	nude	nutmeg
notion	nudge	nutrient

nutriment	nutritive	nuzzled
nutrition	nutritively	nyctalopia
nutritious	nutshell	nymph
nutritiously	nuzzle	nystagmus

O

oaf	objectiveness	obscene
oak	objectivity	obscenity
oaken	objector	obscure
oakum	objurgate	obscured
oar	oblate	obscureness
oarlock	oblation	obscurity
oarsman	obligate	obsequious
oasis	obligation	obsequiously
oaten	obligatory	obsequiousness
oath	oblige	obsequy
oatmeal	obliged	observable
obbligato	obligingly	observance
obduracy	oblique	observant
obdurate	obliquely	observation
obedience	obliqueness	observatory
obedient	obliquity	observe
obeisance	obliterate	observed
obelisk	obliteration	observer
obese	oblivion	observingly
obesity	oblivious	obsess
obey	obliviously	obsession
obituary	obliviousness	obsidian
object	oblong	obsolescence
objection	obloquy	obsolescent
objectionable	obnoxious	obsolete
objective	obnoxiously	obsoletely
objectively	oboe	obsoleteness

obstacle	occasional	octet
obstetrical	occasionally	October
obstetrician	occident	octopus
obstinacy	occidental	ocular
obstinate	occipital	oculist
obstinately	occiput	odd
obstreperous	occlude	oddity
obstruct	occlusion	oddly
obstructed	occult	oddness
obstruction	occultation	odeum
obstructionist	occultism	odious
obstructive	occupancy	odiously
obstructor	occupant	odiousness
obtain	occupation	odium
obtainable	occupied	odometer
obtrude	occupy	odor
obtruded	occur	odoriferous
obtruder	occurred	odorless
obtrusion	occurrence	odorous
obtrusive	ocean	oenology
obtuse	oceanic	of
obtusely	oceanography	off
obtuseness	ocelot	offal
obverse	ocher	offcast
obviate	ochlocracy	offend
obviated	octagon	offense
obviation	octagonal	offensive
obvious	octameter	offer
obviously	octangular	offered
ocarina	octave	offerings
occasion	octavo	offertory

173

offhand	oily	onager
office	ointment	once
officer	okra	one
official	old	oneness
officially	olden	onerous
officiate	old-fashioned	oneself
officiated	oldish	onion
officiation	oldness	onlooker
officious	oldster	only
officiously	oleaginous	onomatopoeia
officiousness	oleander	onslaught
offset	oleate	onto
offshoot	oleomargarine	ontology
offshore	olfactory	onus
often	oligarchy	onward
oftentimes	olive	onyx
ogee	omega	ooze
ogive	omelet	oozed
ogle	omelets	opacity
ogled	omen	opal
ogre	ominous	opalesce
ohm	omission	opalescence
ohmage	omit	opalescent
ohmmeter	omnibus	opaque
oil	omnipotence	open
oiled	omnipotent	opened
oiler	omnipresent	opener
oilily	omniscience	openings
oiliness	omniscient	openly
oilskin	omnivorous	openness
oilstone	on	openwork

174

opera	opprobriously	oratorical
operable	opprobriousness	oratorio
operate	opprobrium	oratory
operated	optic	orb
operatic	optical	orbit
operatically	optician	orchard
operation	optics	orchestra
operative	optimism	orchestral
operator	optimist	orchestrate
operetta	optimistic	orchestrated
ophthalmology	optimistically	orchestration
opiate	optimists	orchid
opinion	optimum	orchidaceous
opinionated	option	ordain
opinionative	optional	ordained
opium	optionally	ordeal
opossum	optometrist	orderliness
opponent	optometry	orderly
opportune	opulence	ordinal
opportunity	opulent	ordinance
oppose	opus	ordinarily
opposed	or	ordinary
opposite	oracle	ordination
opposition	oracular	ordnance
oppress	oracularly	organ
oppression	oral	organic
oppressive	orally	organically
oppressively	orange	organism
oppressiveness	orangeade	organist
oppressor	oration	organization
opprobrious	orator	organize

orgy	orphanage	ostracize
orient	orphanhood	ostracized
oriental	orrery	ostrich
orientalism	orthodox	otalgia
orientalist	orthoëpy	other
orientate	orthography	otherwise
orientation	orthopedic	otiose
orifice	ortolan	otitis
origin	oscillate	otorrhea
original	oscillated	otter
originality	oscillation	ottoman
originally	oscillator	ought
originate	oscillatory	ounce
originated	osculate	our
origination	osculation	ours
originative	osculatory	ourselves
originator	osier	oust
oriole	osmium	ouster
Orion	osmosis	out
orlop	osprey	outcast
ormolu	osseous	outclass
ornament	ossification	outcome
ornamental	ossify	outcrop
ornamentally	ostensible	outcroppings
ornamentation	ostensibly	outcry
ornate	ostentation	outcurve
ornithological	ostentatious	outdistance
ornithologist	ostentatiously	outdo
ornithology	osteopath	outdoors
orotund	osteopathy	outer
orphan	ostracism	outermost

176

outfield	outside	overconfident
outfit	outsider	overdevelop
outfitter	outsize	overdo
outflank	outskirt	overdose
outgo	outstandingly	overdraft
outgrowth	outstay	overdress
outings	outstrip	overdriven
outlandish	outtalk	overdue
outlandishness	outward	overestimate
outlast	outwardly	overexpose
outlaw	outwear	overexposure
outlay	outwit	overflow
outlet	oval	overgrown
outlets	ovation	overhand
outline	oven	overhang
outlive	over	overhaul
outlook	overalls	overhead
outmarch	overanxious	overheat
outnumber	overawe	overindulge
outrage	overbalance	overindulgence
outraged	overbear	overissue
outrageous	overbid	overlap
outrageously	overboard	overload
outrageousness	overburden	overlook
outrank	overcapitalize	overlord
outreach	overcast	overmaster
outrider	overcautious	overnight
outrigger	overcharge	overpay
outright	overclothes	overpowered
outrun	overcoat	overpoweringly
outset	overcome	overproduction

177

overrate	overstrain	owe
overrated	oversubscribe	owed
overreach	oversupply	owl
override	overt	owlet
overripe	overtake	owlets
overrule	overthrow	owlish
overrun	overtime	own
overseas	overtone	owned
overseer	overture	owner
overshadow	overturn	ownership
overshadowed	overturned	oxalate
overshoe	overvalue	oxalic
oversight	overweight	oxidation
oversize	overwhelm	oxide
overspread	overwhelmed	oxidize
overstate	overwhelmingly	oxygen
overstatement	overwork	oxyhydrogen
overstep	overwrought	oyster
overstock	ovum	ozone

P

pabulum
pace
pacemaker
pacer
pachyderm
pacific
pacification
pacifier
pacifism
pacifist
pacify
pack
package
packer
packet
packings
packsaddle
pact
pad
paddle
paddled
paddock
padlock
pagan
paganism
page
pageant

pageantry
pagination
pagoda
paid
pail
pain
painful
painless
painstaking
paint
painted
painter
pair
paired
pairings
pajama
palace
palanquin
palatability
palatable
palate
palatial
palatially
palatinate
pale
paleography
palette

palfrey
palimpsest
palindrome
palings
palisade
pall
palladium
pallbearer
palliate
palliated
palliation
palliative
pallid
pallium
pallor
palm
palmetto
palmist
palmistry
palpability
palpable
palpate
palpation
palpitant
palpitate
palpitatingly
palpitation

palsied	pantheon	paralyze
palsy	panther	paralyzed
paltry	pantograph	paramount
pampas	pantomime	paranoia
pamper	pantry	paranoiac
pamphlet	papacy	parapet
pamphlets	papal	paraphernalia
panacea	paper	paraphrase
pancake	papered	paraplegia
panchromatic	papeterie	paraplegic
pancreas	papoose	parasite
pancreatic	paprika	parasitic
panda	parable	parasitical
pandemic	parabola	parasiticide
pandemonium	parabolic	parasol
pander	parabolical	parboil
pandered	parachute	parcel
panegyric	parade	parceled
panegyrical	paradigm	parch
panegyrize	paradise	parchment
panel	paradox	pardon
paneled	paradoxical	pardonable
pang	paraffin	pardoned
panic	paragon	pare
pannier	paragraph	pared
pannikin	parallax	paregoric
panorama	parallel	parent
panoramic	paralleled	parentage
pansy	parallelogram	parental
pant	paralysis	parentheses
pantaloon	paralytic	parenthesis

parenthetical	parsnip	paschal
parenthetically	parsonage	pass
parenthood	part	passable
parietal	partake	passage
parings	parted	passageway
parish	parterre	passbook
parishioner	partial	passed
parity	partiality	passenger
park	partially	passion
parka	participant	passionate
parkway	participate	passionately
parlance	participated	passionless
parley	participation	passive
parliament	participator	passivity
parliamentarian	participial	passover
parliamentary	participle	passport
parlor	particle	password
parochial	particular	past
parody	particularity	paste
parole	particularize	pasteboard
paroxysm	particularized	pastel
paroxysmal	particularly	pastern
parquet	partisan	pasteurized
parricidal	partisanship	pastime
parricide	partition	pastor
parrot	partitioned	pastoral
parry	partner	pastorate
parse	partnership	pastrami
parsimonious	partridge	pastry
parsimony	party	pasturage
parsley	parvenu	patch

181

patchwork	patriotic	pawnbroker
patchy	patriotically	pawned
patella	patriotism	pawnshop
patellar	patrol	pay
patent	patrolled	payable
patentable	patrolman	payee
patented	patron	payer
patentee	patronage	paymaster
paternal	patroness	payment
paternalism	patronize	pea
paternally	patronized	peace
paternity	patronymic	peaceable
path	patter	peaceably
pathetic	pattered	peaceful
pathless	pattern	peacemaker
pathologist	patterned	peach
pathology	paucity	peacock
pathos	Paulist	peak
pathway	pauper	peaked
patience	pauperism	peal
patient	pauperization	pealed
patina	pauperize	peanut
patio	pause	pear
patness	paused	pearl
patriarch	pave	pearlite
patriarchal	paved	pearly
patriarchate	pavement	peasant
patrician	pavilion	peasantry
patrimonial	paw	peat
patrimony	pawl	peavey
patriot	pawn	pebble

182

pebbled	pediatrics	peltry
pebbly	pedicular	pelvic
pecan	pediculosis	pelvis
peccadillo	pedigree	pemmican
peccancy	pedigreed	pen
peccant	pediment	penal
peccary	pedometer	penalization
peck	peek	penalize
pectase	peel	penalized
pectin	peeled	penalty
pectoral	peelings	penance
peculate	peep	penchant
peculiar	peer	pencil
peculiarity	peerage	penciled
peculiarly	peered	pendant
pecuniary	peeress	pendency
pedagogic	peerless	pending
pedagogical	peevish	pendulous
pedagogue	peg	pendulum
pedagogy	Pegasus	penetrability
pedal	pelagic	penetrable
pedant	pelf	penetrant
pedantic	pelican	penetrate
pedantical	pelisse	penetration
pedantry	pellagra	penetrative
peddle	pellet	penguin
peddler	pellets	penholder
pedestal	pellucid	penicillin
pedestrian	pelota	penicillium
pedestrianism	pelt	peninsula
pediatrician	pelted	peninsular

183

penitence
penitent
penitential
penitentiary
penitently
penknife
penman
penmanship
pennant
penniless
penny
penologist
penology
pension
pensionary
pensioner
pensive
penstock
pent
pentagon
pentameter
Pentateuch
pentathlon
Pentecost
penthouse
penult
penultimate
penumbra
penurious
penury
peon

peony
people
peplum
pepper
pepperiness
peppermint
peppery
pepsin
peptic
peradventure
perambulate
perambulator
perborate
percale
perceivable
perceive
per cent
percentage
percentile
perceptibility
perceptible
perception
perceptive
perceptual
perch
perchance
percipiency
percipient
percolate
percolation
percolator

percussion
percussive
peregrination
peremptorily
peremptoriness
peremptory
perennial
perfect
perfectibility
perfectible
perfection
perfectly
perfidious
perfidy
perforate
perforation
perforator
perforce
perform
performable
performance
performed
performer
perfume
perfumed
perfumer
perfumery
perfunctory
pergola
perhaps
peril

perilous	permeation	persecutor
perilously	permissibility	perseverance
perimeter	permissible	persevere
period	permission	persevered
periodate	permissive	persiflage
periodic	permit	persimmon
periodical	permitted	persist
periodicity	permutation	persistence
peripatetic	permutite	persistency
peripheral	pernicious	persistent
periphery	peroration	persists
periphrastic	peroxide	person
periscope	perpendicular	personable
perish	perpetrate	personage
perishable	perpetration	personal
peristyle	perpetrator	personality
peritoneum	perpetual	personalize
peritonitis	perpetually	personally
periwinkle	perpetuate	personalty
perjure	perpetuated	personification
perjured	perpetuation	personify
perjurer	perpetuator	personnel
perjury	perpetuity	perspective
permanence	perplex	perspicacious
permanent	perplexed	perspicacity
permanently	perplexedly	perspicuous
permanganate	perplexingly	perspiration
permeability	perplexity	perspiratory
permeable	perquisite	perspire
permeate	persecute	perspired
permeated	persecution	persuade

185

persuaded	pessimist	petulant
persuader	pessimistic	petunia
persuasion	pessimists	pew
persuasive	pester	pewter
persuasiveness	pesthouse	phaeton
persulphate	pestiferous	phalanges
pert	pestilence	phalanx
pertain	pestilent	phantasm
pertinacious	pestilential	phantom
pertinacity	pestle	pharmaceutic
pertinence	pet	pharmaceutical
pertinency	petal	pharmacist
pertinent	petaliferous	pharmacology
perturb	petard	pharmacopoeia
perturbable	petite	pharmacy
perturbation	petition	pharyngitis
perusal	petitioner	pharynx
peruse	petrel	phase
perused	petrifaction	pheasant
Peruvian	petrifactive	phenol
pervade	petrify	phenomena
pervasion	petrol	phenomenal
pervasive	petrolatum	phenomenology
perverse	petroleum	phenomenon
perversion	petrology	phial
perversity	petticoat	philander
perversive	pettily	philanderer
pervert	pettiness	philanthropic
perverted	pettish	philanthropical
pervious	petty	philanthropist
pessimism	petulance	philanthropy

186

philately	phosphorescence	physiology
philatelic	phosphorescent	physique
philatelist	phosphoric	pianist
philharmonic	phosphorus	piano
philippic	photoelectric	piazza
Philippine	photoengraving	pica
Philistine	photogenic	picaresque
philologist	photograph	piccolo
philology	photographer	pick
philosopher	photographic	pickax
philosophic	photography	picker
philosophical	photogravure	pickerel
philosophize	photolith-ograph	picket
philosophy	photomi-crograph	pickle
philter	photoplay	picklock
phlebitis	photostat	pickpocket
phlebotomy	phrase	pickup
phlegm	phrased	picnic
phlegmatic	phraseology	picnicker
phlox	phrenetic	picric
phobia	phrenic	pictograph
phone	phrenologist	pictorial
phonetic	phrenology	pictorially
phonetician	phthisis	picture
phonetics	phylactery	pictured
phonic	physic	picturesque
phonograph	physical	pie
phosphate	physically	piece
phosphide	physician	piecemeal
phosphite	physics	piecework
phosphoresce	physiognomy	pied

187

pieplant	pillory	pipe
pier	pillow	pipette
pierce	pillowcase	piquancy
pierced	pilot	piquant
piety	pimento	pique
pig	pimple	piracy
pigeon	pin	piragua
pigeonhole	pinafore	pirate
piggery	pincers	pirated
piggish	pinch	piratic
pigheaded	pincushion	piratical
pigment	pine	pirogue
pigmentation	pineapple	pirouette
pigmy	pinfeather	piscatology
pigskin	pinfish	piscatorial
pigsty	ping-pong	pistachio
pigtail	pinguid	pistol
pigwood	pinhole	piston
pike	pinion	pit
piker	pink	pitch
pikestaff	pinnace	pitcher
pilaster	pinnacle	piteous
pilchard	pinochle	piteousness
pile	pinto	pitfall
piled	pinweed	pith
pilfer	pioneer	pithily
pilgrim	pioneered	pithiness
pilgrimage	pious	pithy
pillage	piously	pitiable
pillar	pip	pitiful
pillion	pipage	pitiless

pitilessly	plainly	plateau
pitilessness	plainness	plated
pittance	plaint	plateful
pitted	plaintiff	platen
pituitary	plaintive	plater
pity	plan	platform
pityingly	planchette	platina
pivot	plane	platinate
pivotal	planet	platinic
placability	planetaria	platiniferous
placable	planetarium	platinoid
placard	planetary	platinum
placate	planetoid	platitude
placated	plangent	platitudinize
placatory	plank	platitudinous
place	planked	platoon
placebo	plankton	platter
placeman	planned	platypus
placement	plant	plaudit
placer	plantain	plausibility
placid	plantation	plausible
placidity	planted	play
placidly	planter	player
placket	plantings	playful
plagiarism	plasma	playfulness
plagiarist	plaster	playgoer
plagiarize	plastered	playground
plagiary	plasterer	playings
plague	plastic	playmate
plaid	plasticity	plaything
plain	plate	playtime

189

playwright
plaza
plea
plead
pleader
pleadingly
pleadings
pleasant
pleasantly
pleasantness
pleasantry
please
pleasurable
pleasure
plebeian
plebiscite
plectrum
pledge
pledgee
pledger
pledget
pledgor
plenary
plenarily
plenipotentiary
plenitude
plenteous
plentiful
plenty
plenum
pleonasm

pleonastic
plethora
plethoric
pleura
pleurisy
plexus
pliability
pliable
pliably
pliancy
pliant
plier
pliers
plight
plinth
plodder
plot
plotted
plotter
plough
plover
plow
plowboy
plowman
plowshare
pluck
pluckily
plucky
plug
plugged
plum

plumage
plumb
plumbago
plumbate
plumber
plumbic
plumbous
plume
plumed
plummet
plump
plumper
plumpest
plumply
plumpness
plunder
plundered
plunderer
plunge
plunged
plunger
plunk
plural
plurality
pluralize
plus
plush
plutocracy
plutocrat
plutocratic
plutonic

pluvial	poise	politician
ply	poised	politicly
pneumatic	poison	politics
pneumatically	poisoned	polity
pneumatics	poisoner	polka
pneumonia	poisonous	poll
poach	poke	pollen
poacher	poker	pollinate
pocket	pokeweed	pollination
pocketbook	polar	polliniferous
pocketknife	polarity	pollute
pockmark	polarization	polluted
pod	polarize	pollution
podagra	polarized	polo
podiatry	polarizer	polonaise
poem	pole	polonium
poet	polecat	poltroon
poetaster	polemic	polyandrous
poetic	polemical	polyandry
poetical	polemicist	polychrome
poetry	police	polyclinic
poignancy	policeman	polygamist
poignant	policy	polygamous
poinciana	polish	polygamy
poinsettia	polisher	polyglot
point	polite	polygon
pointed	politely	polygonal
pointedly	politeness	polymeric
pointer	politic	polyp
pointless	political	polyphony
pointlessly	politically	polysyllabic

191

polytechnic	poorness	portal
pomade	popcorn	portcullis
pommel	poplar	portend
pomology	poplin	portent
pomp	poppet	portentous
pompadour	poppy	porter
pompano	populace	porterhouse
pomposity	popular	portfolio
pompous	popularity	porthole
poncho	popularization	portico
pond	popularize	portiere
ponder	popularized	portion
ponderable	popularly	portrait
pondered	populate	portraiture
ponderous	populated	portray
pondweed	population	portrayal
pongee	populous	Portuguese
poniard	porcelain	portulaca
pontiff	porch	pose
pontifically	porcupine	poses
pontificate	pore	position
pontoon	pork	positive
pony	pornography	posse
poodle	porosity	possess
pool	porous	possession
pooled	porphyry	possessive
poor	porpoise	possessor
poorer	porringer	possessorship
poorest	port	possibility
poorhouse	portable	possible
poorly	portage	possum

post	pot	poundings
postage	potable	pour
postal	potash	pout
postdate	potassium	poverty
postdated	potation	powder
poster	potato	powdered
posterior	potboiler	powdery
posterity	potency	power
postern	potent	powerful
postgraduate	potentate	powerfully
posthaste	potential	powerless
posthumous	potentiality	powerlessly
postilion	potentially	powerlessness
postlude	pothole	powwow
postman	pothook	practicability
postmark	potion	practicable
postmaster	potlatch	practicably
postoperative	potluck	practical
postpaid	potpie	practicality
postpone	potpourri	practically
postponed	potsherd	practice
postponement	pottage	practitioner
postprandial	potter	pragmatic
postscript	pottery	pragmatism
postulant	pouch	pragmatist
postulate	poultice	prairie
postulation	poultry	praise
posture	pounce	praised
postured	pound	praiseworthy
posturings	poundage	praline
posy	poundcake	prance

193

prank
prate
pratique
prattle
prawn
pray
prayer
prayerful
prayerfully
preach
preacher
preachment
preamble
prearrange
prearrangement
prebendary
precanceled
precarious
precaution
precautionary
precede
preceded
precedence
precedent
precept
preceptor
preceptress
precinct
precious
preciously
precipice

precipitancy
precipitant
precipitate
precipitately
precipitation
precipitous
precise
precision
preclude
preclusion
precocious
precociously
precocity
preconceived
preconception
precursor
precursory
predaceous
predacity
predatory
predecease
predecessor
predestination
predestine
predeterminate
predetermine
prediastolic
predicament
predicate
predicated
predication

predict
predictable
prediction
predictive
predigest
predigestion
predilection
predispose
predisposed
predisposition
predominant
predominate
pre-eminence
pre-eminent
pre-empt
pre-emption
preen
preface
prefaced
prefatory
prefect
prefer
preferable
preferably
preference
preferential
preferentially
preferment
preferred
prefix
preform

pregnancy	prepared	presently
pregnant	preparedness	presentment
prehensile	prepay	preservation
prehistoric	prepayment	preservative
prejudge	preponderance	preserve
prejudice	preponderant	preserver
prejudiced	preponderate	preside
prejudicial	preponderatingly	presidency
prejudicially	preposition	president
prelate	prepositional	presidential
preliminary	prepossess	press
prelude	prepossession	pressboard
premature	preposterous	pressman
premeditate	prerequisite	pressure
premeditated	prerogative	presswork
premeditation	presage	prestidigitator
premier	presbyter	prestige
premise	presbyterian	presto
premises	presbytery	presumable
premium	prescience	presumably
premonition	prescient	presume
premonitory	prescribe	presumed
prenatal	prescribed	presumedly
preoccupation	prescription	presumption
preoccupied	prescriptive	presumptive
preoccupy	presence	presumptuous
prepaid	present	presuppose
preparation	presentability	presystolic
preparative	presentable	pretend
preparatory	presentation	pretended
prepare	presentiment	pretender

195

pretense	prey	primogeniture
pretension	price	primordial
pretensions	priced	primrose
pretentious	prices	prince
preterit	priceless	princeliness
preternatural	prick	princely
pretext	prickle	princes
pretexts	prickliness	princess
prettier	prickly	principal
prettiest	pride	principality
prettily	prideful	principally
prettiness	priest	principle
pretty	priestess	print
pretzel	priesthood	printable
prevail	priestly	printed
prevailed	priggish	printer
prevalence	prim	printery
prevalent	primacy	printings
prevalently	primal	prior
prevaricate	primarily	priority
prevarication	primary	priory
prevaricator	primate	prism
prevent	primateship	prismatic
preventability	prime	prison
preventable	primed	prisoner
prevented	primer	pristine
prevention	primer	privacy
preventive	primeval	private
preview	primitive	privateer
previous	primly	privately
prevision	primness	privateness

196

privation	proclamation	profess
privet	proclivity	professed
privilege	proconsul	professedly
privily	procrastinate	profession
privity	procrastination	professional
privy	procrastinator	professionalism
prize	proctor	professionally
prized	procurable	professor
probability	procuration	professorial
probable	procurator	professorship
probably	procure	proffer
probate	procured	proficiency
probation	procurement	proficient
probationary	prodigal	proficiently
probe	prodigality	profile
probity	prodigious	profit
problem	prodigiously	profitable
problematic	prodigy	profitably
proboscis	produce	profiteer
procedural	produced	profitless
procedure	producer	profligacy
proceed	produces	profligate
proceeded	product	profound
proceedings	production	profoundness
process	productive	profundity
processed	productivity	profuse
processes	proem	profusely
procession	profanation	profuseness
processional	profanatory	profusion
proclaim	profane	progenitor
proclaimed	profanity	progeny

197

prognosis	promiscuity	pronunciation
prognostic	promiscuous	proof
prognosticate	promiscuously	prop
prognostication	promiscuousness	propaganda
program	promise	propagandist
progress	promisingly	propagate
progression	promissory	propagated
progressive	promontory	propagation
prohibit	promote	propane
prohibition	promoted	propel
prohibitionist	promoter	propellant
prohibitory	promotion	propelled
project	prompt	propeller
projectile	prompted	propensity
projection	prompter	proper
projector	promptitude	properly
proletarian	promptly	properties
proletariat	promptness	property
proliferate	promulgate	prophecy
proliferation	promulgation	prophesied
prolific	pronate	prophesy
prolix	pronation	prophet
prolixity	prone	prophetic
prologue	prong	prophetically
prolong	pronghorn	prophylactic
prolongate	pronominal	prophylaxis
prolongation	pronoun	propinquity
prolonged	pronounce	propitiate
promenade	pronounceable	propitiated
prominence	pronounced	propitiation
prominent	pronouncement	propitiatory

propitious
proponent
proportion
proportionable
proportional
proportionally
proportionate
proportionately
proposal
propose
proposed
proposition
propound
proprietary
proprietor
propriety
proptosis
propulsion
prorate
prorogation
prorogue
prorogued
prosaic
proscenium
proscribe
proscribed
proscription
prose
prosecute
prosecuted
prosecution

prosecutor
proselyte
proselytize
prosily
prosiness
prosody
prospect
prospective
prospector
prospectus
prosper
prosperity
prosperous
prosperously
prosthesis
prosthetic
prostrate
prostration
prosy
protagonist
protagonists
protean
protect
protected
protectingly
protection
protectionist
protective
protectively
protectiveness
protector

protectorate
protein
protest
protestant
protestation
protestingly
protests
prothonotary
protocol
protoplasm
prototype
protoxide
protozoa
protract
protraction
protractive
protractor
protrude
protruded
protrusion
protrusive
protuberance
protuberant
proud
prouder
proudest
proudly
provable
prove
provender
proverb

199

proverbial
provide
provided
providence
provident
providential
providentially
provider
province
provincial
provincialism
provinciality
provincially
provision
provisional
proviso
provisory
provocation
provocative
provoke
provokingly
provost
prow
prowess
prowl
proximal
proximate
proximity
proximo
proxy
prude

prudence
prudent
prudential
prudentially
prudently
prudery
prudish
prune
pruned
prurience
prurient
Prussian
pry
pryingly
psalm
psalmist
Psalter
pseudonym
psoriasis
psychiatric
psychiatrist
psychiatry
psychic
psychical
psychoanalysis
psychological
psychologist
psychology
psychopathic
psychopathology
psychosis

ptomaine
public
publication
publicist
publicity
publicly
publish
publisher
puce
puck
pucker
pudding
puddle
puddled
puddler
pudency
pudginess
pudgy
pueblo
puerile
puerility
puff
puffin
puffiness
puffy
pug
pugilism
pugilist
pugilistic
pugnacious
pugnaciously

pugnacity	puncheon	purchasable
puissance	punctilio	purchase
puissant	punctilious	purchased
pull	punctiliously	purchaser
pulled	punctiliousness	pure
pullet	punctual	purely
pulley	punctuality	purer
Pullman	punctually	purest
pullulate	punctuate	purgative
pulmonary	punctuated	purgatory
pulmotor	punctuation	purge
pulp	puncture	purification
pulpiness	punctured	purifier
pulpit	pung	purify
pulpiteer	pungency	purism
pulpy	pungent	purist
pulsate	puniness	puritan
pulsated	punish	puritanic
pulsation	punishable	puritanical
pulsator	punishment	Puritanism
pulsatory	punitive	purity
pulse	punk	purl
pulverization	puny	purlieu
pulverize	pup	purloin
pulverizer	pupa	purple
pumice	pupae	purplish
pump	pupil	purport
pumpernickel	puppet	purported
pumpkin	puppetry	purpose
pun	puppy	purposeful
punch	purblind	purposeless

201

purposely	push	puzzle
purr	pushcart	puzzled
purse	pusher	puzzler
purser	pusillanimous	pyelitis
purslane	pustulant	pyemia
pursuance	pustular	pygmy
pursuant	pustulate	pylon
pursue	pustulation	pylorus
pursued	pustule	pyonephrosis
pursuit	put	pyorrhea
pursuivant	putative	pyramid
pursy	putrefaction	pyramidal
purulence	putrefactive	pyre
purulency	putrefy	pyrexia
purulent	putrescence	pyrites
purvey	putrescent	pyrography
purveyance	putrid	pyrometer
purveyor	putt	pyrotechnics
purview	putter	pyroxylin
pus	putty	python

Q

quack	qualities	quaver
quackery	quality	quavered
quadrangle	qualm	quay
quadratic	quandary	quayage
quadratics	quantitative	queen
quadrature	quantities	queenly
quadrennial	quantity	queer
quadrennially	quantum	quell
quadrilateral	quarantine	quelled
quadrille	quarrel	quench
quadruped	quarreled	quenchless
quadruple	quarrelsome	querulous
quadruplex	quarry	query
quadruplicate	quart	quest
quaff	quartan	question
quagmire	quarter	questionable
quahog	quartered	questioner
quail	quarterly	questionnaire
quailed	quartermaster	queue
quaint	quartet	quibble
quaintly	quartile	quick
quaintness	quarto	quicken
Quaker	quartz	quickened
qualification	quash	quicklime
qualified	quasi	quickly
qualify	quaternary	quickness
qualitative	quatrain	quicksand

203

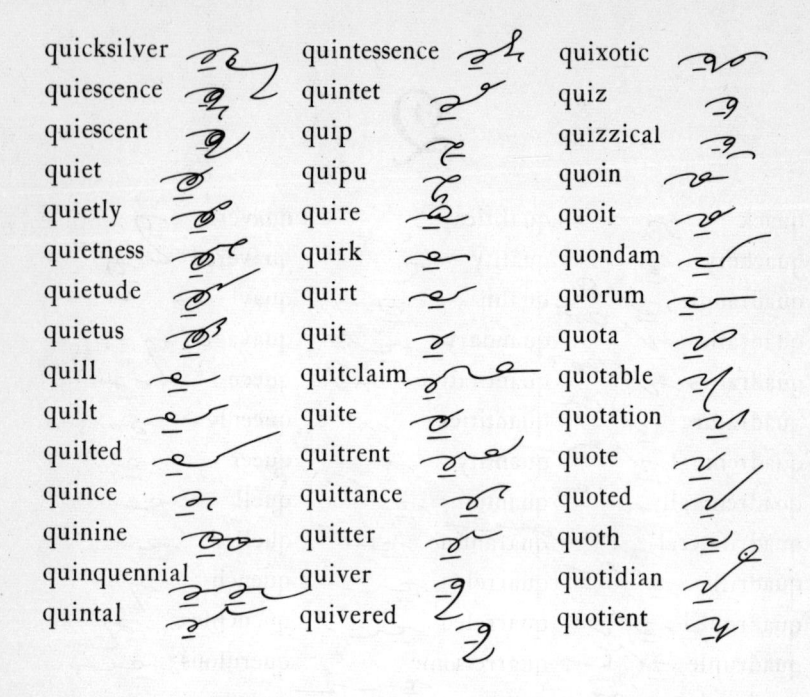

quicksilver	quintessence	quixotic
quiescence	quintet	quiz
quiescent	quip	quizzical
quiet	quipu	quoin
quietly	quire	quoit
quietness	quirk	quondam
quietude	quirt	quorum
quietus	quit	quota
quill	quitclaim	quotable
quilt	quite	quotation
quilted	quitrent	quote
quince	quittance	quoted
quinine	quitter	quoth
quinquennial	quiver	quotidian
quintal	quivered	quotient

R

rabbet
rabbinical
rabbit
rabbitry
rabble
rabid
rabidly
rabies
raccoon
race
raced
racer
raceway
rachitic
rachitis
racial
racially
racily
raciness
rack
racket
raconteur
radial
radially
radiance
radiancy
radiant

radiantly
radiate
radiated
radiation
radiator
radical
radicalism
radically
radii
radio
radiogram
radiophone
radish
radium
radius
radiuses
radon
raffia
raffle
raffled
raft
rafter
raftsman
rag
ragamuffin
rage
ragged

raglan
ragout
ragpicker
ragtime
ragweed
raid
rail
railed
railhead
railings
raillery
railroad
railway
raiment
rain
rainbow
raincoat
rainfall
rainstorm
rainy
raise
raisin
rajah
rake
rakish
rally
ram

205

ramble	rantingly	rat
rambled	rapacious	ratchet
rambler	rapaciously	rate
ramekin	rapacity	rated
ramification	rapid	rather
ramify	rapidity	rathskeller
rammed	rapidly	ratification
ramp	rapier	ratify
rampage	rapine	ratings
rampant	rapport	ratio
rampart	rapt	ratiocination
ramrod	raptorial	ratiocinative
ramshackle	rapture	ration
ranch	rapturous	rational
rancher	rapturously	rationalism
ranchman	rapturousness	rationalistic
rancho	rarefaction	rationalization
rancid	rarefy	rationalize
rancidity	rarely	rationalized
rancidly	rareness	rationally
rancor	rarity	rationed
rancorous	rascal	ratline
random	rascality	rattan
range	rascally	ratter
ranger	rash	rattle
rank	rasher	rattled
ranked	rashest	rattler
rankle	rashly	rattlesnake
ransack	rashness	rattly
ransom	rasp	raucous
rant	raspberry	ravage

206

ravaged
rave
ravel
raveled
raven
ravenous
ravine
ravish
ravished
ravishment
raw
rawboned
rawhide
rawness
ray
rayless
rayon
raze
razed
razor
razorback
reach
react
reaction
reactionary
read
readability
readable
reader
readily
readiness

readings
readjust
readjustment
readmission
readmit
ready
reaffirm
reaffirmation
reagent
real
realism
realist
realistic
realistically
reality
realizable
realization
realize
realized
really
realm
realtor
realty
ream
reamer
reanimate
reap
reaper
reappear
reappearance
reappoint

reappointment
rear
reared
reargue
rearm
rearmament
rearmed
rearmost
rearrange
rearrangement
rearward
reason
reasonable
reasonableness
reasonably
reassemble
reassert
reasserted
reassign
reassigned
reassume
reassumed
reassurance
reassure
reassured
rebate
rebated
rebel
rebellion
rebellious
rebind

rebirth	receiver	reck
reborn	receivership	reckless
rebound	recent	reckon
rebuff	recently	reckoned
rebuild	receptacle	reckoner
rebuilt	receptive	reclaim
rebuke	receptively	reclaimable
rebukingly	receptiveness	reclaimed
rebus	receptivity	reclamation
rebut	recess	recline
rebuttal	recesses	reclined
rebutter	recession	recluse
recalcitrant	recessional	recognition
recall	recessive	recognizable
recalled	recharge	recognizance
recant	recidivism	recognize
recanted	recipe	recognized
recapitalization	recipient	recoil
recapitalize	reciprocal	recoiled
recapitulate	reciprocally	recollect
recapitulated	reciprocate	recollected
recapitulation	reciprocation	recollection
recapture	reciprocative	recommence
recast	reciprocator	recommend
recede	reciprocity	recommendation
receded	recital	recommendatory
receipt	recitalist	recommended
receipted	recitation	recommit
receivable	recitative	recompense
receive	recite	reconcilable
received	recited	reconcile

reconciled
reconcilement
reconciliation
reconciliatory
recondite
reconnaissance
reconnoiter
reconnoitered
reconquer
reconquered
reconsider
reconstitute
reconstruct
reconstruction
reconstructive
record
recorded
recorder
recordings
recount
recounted
recoup
recoupment
recourse
recover
recoverable
recovery
recreant
recreation
recriminate
recrimination

recriminative
recriminatory
recrudescence
recrudescent
recruit
recruitment
recrystallize
rectal
rectangle
rectangular
rectification
rectifier
rectify
rectilinear
rectitude
rector
rectory
recumbency
recumbent
recuperate
recuperated
recuperation
recuperative
recuperatory
recur
recurred
recurrence
recurrent
recusant
red
redbreast

redden
redder
reddest
reddish
redeem
redeemed
redeemer
redemption
redemptory
redirect
redirected
rediscount
rediscover
redistribute
redistribution
redness
redolence
redolent
redouble
redoubt
redoubtable
redound
redress
reduce
reduced
reducer
reducible
reduction
redundance
redundancy
redundant

209

re-echo	refined	refreshingly
reed	refinement	refreshment
reediness	refiner	refrigerant
reedy	refinery	refrigerate
reef	refit	refrigerated
reefer	reflect	refrigeration
reel	reflected	refrigerative
re-elect	reflection	refrigerator
re-embark	reflective	refuge
re-embarkation	reflector	refugee
re-enact	reflex	refulgence
re-enforce	reflexes	refulgent
re-enforcement	reflexive	refund
re-engage	reforestation	refunded
re-engrave	reform	refurnish
re-enlist	reformation	refusal
re-enter	reformative	refuse
re-entry	reformatory	refused
re-establish	reformed	refuses
re-examination	reformer	refutation
re-examine	refract	refute
re-export	refracted	refuted
re-exportation	refraction	regain
refectory	refractive	regained
refer	refractivity	regal
referable	refractor	regale
referee	refractory	regaled
reference	refrain	regalement
referendum	refrained	regalia
referred	refresh	regally
refine	refresher	regard

regardful	regretfulness	reinsure
regardless	regrettable	reintroduce
regards	regretted	reinvest
regatta	regular	reinvigorate
regency	regularity	reinvigoration
regeneracy	regularly	reissue
regenerate	regulate	reiterate
regeneration	regulated	reiteration
regenerative	regulates	reiterative
regenerator	regulation	reject
regent	regulator	rejected
regicide	regurgitate	rejection
regimen	regurgitation	rejoice
regiment	rehabilitate	rejoiced
regimental	rehabilitation	rejoices
regimentals	rehearsal	rejoin
regimentation	rehearse	rejoinder
region	reign	rejuvenate
regional	reimburse	rejuvenation
regionally	reimbursed	rejuvenescent
register	reimbursement	rekindle
registered	reimport	relapse
registrar	reimportation	relapsed
registration	rein	relate
registry	reincarnate	related
regress	reincarnation	relation
regression	reindeer	relational
regressive	reinsert	relationship
regret	reinstall	relative
regretful	reinstate	relatively
regretfully	reinsurance	relativity

relator	relish	remittal
relax	relive	remittance
relaxation	reload	remitted
relaxed	relucent	remittent
relaxes	reluctance	remitter
relay	reluctant	remnant
release	reluctantly	remodel
released	rely	remonetize
relegate	remain	remonstrance
relegated	remainder	remonstrant
relegation	remained	remonstrate
relent	remake	remonstrated
relented	remand	remonstration
relentless	remark	remonstrative
relevance	remarkable	remorse
relevancy	remarry	remorseful
relevant	remediable	remorsefully
reliability	remedial	remorseless
reliable	remedied	remote
reliance	remedy	remoteness
reliant	remember	remount
relic	remembered	removability
relief	remembrance	removable
relievable	remind	removal
relieve	reminder	remove
religion	remindful	remunerate
religious	reminiscence	remuneration
religiously	reminiscent	remunerative
relinquish	remiss	renaissance
relinquishment	remission	renal
reliquary	remit	render

212

rendered
rendezvous
rendition
renegade
renew
renewable
renewal
renewed
rennet
renominate
renominated
renounce
renovate
renovated
renovation
renown
renowned
rent
rental
rented
renumber
renunciation
renunciatory
reopen
reorder
reorganization
reorganize
reorient
repaid
repair
repaired

reparable
reparation
reparative
repartee
repast
repatriate
repay
repayment
repeal
repealed
repeat
repeatedly
repeater
repel
repelled
repellence
repellent
repent
repentance
repentant
repented
repercussion
repercussive
repertoire
repertory
repetition
repetitious
repetitive
rephrase
repine
repined

replace
replaced
replacement
replant
replenish
replenishment
replete
repletion
replevin
replica
replied
reply
report
reported
reporter
repose
reposed
reposeful
repository
repossess
repossessed
reprehend
reprehensible
reprehension
reprehensive
represent
representation
representative
repress
repression
repressive

213

reprieve	repugnant	resemblance
reprimand	repulse	resemble
reprimandingly	repulsed	resent
reprint	repulsion	resented
reprinted	repulsive	resentful
reprisal	repurchase	resentfully
reproach	reputable	resentfulness
reproachful	reputation	resentment
reproachfully	repute	reservation
reproachfulness	reputed	reserve
reprobate	reputedly	reserved
reprobation	request	reservist
reproduce	requests	reservoir
reproducer	requiem	resettle
reproduction	require	resettlement
reproductive	requirement	reship
reproof	requires	reshipment
reprove	requisite	reside
reproved	requisition	residence
reprovingly	requital	residency
reptile	requite	resident
reptilian	reredos	residential
republic	rerun	residual
republican	resale	residuary
republicanism	rescind	residue
republicanize	rescinded	residuum
republish	rescript	resign
repudiate	rescue	resignation
repudiated	rescued	resigned
repudiation	research	resignedly
repugnance	resection	resiliency

resilient	respectable	restive
resin	respected	restively
resist	respecter	restiveness
resistance	respective	restless
resistant	respects	restock
resistible	respirable	restoration
resistivity	respiration	restorative
resistless	respirator	restore
resists	respiratory	restored
resoluble	respire	restrain
resolute	respite	restrained
resoluteness	resplendence	restrainingly
resolution	resplendency	restraint
resolvable	resplendent	restrict
resolve	respond	restricted
resolved	responded	restriction
resolvent	respondent	restrictive
resonance	response	rests
resonant	responsibility	result
resonate	responsible	resultant
resonator	responsive	resumable
resort	rest	resume
resorted	restate	resumed
resound	restatement	resumption
resounded	restaurant	resurface
resoundingly	restaurateur	resurgence
resource	rested	resurgent
resourceful	restful	resurrect
resourcefulness	restfully	resurrected
respect	restfulness	resurrection
respectability	restitution	resuscitate

215

resuscitated
resuscitation
resuscitative
retail
retailed
retailer
retain
retained
retainer
retake
retaliate
retaliated
retaliation
retaliative
retaliatory
retard
retardation
retarded
retch
retell
retention
retentive
retentivity
reticence
reticent
reticle
reticular
reticulate
reticule
retina
retinal

retinitis
retinue
retire
retired
retirement
retold
retort
retorted
retouch
retoucher
retrace
retraceable
retract
retracted
retractile
retraction
retractive
retractor
retread
retreat
retreated
retrench
retrenchment
retrial
retribution
retributive
retrievable
retrieve
retrieved
retriever
retroactive

retroactivity
retrocession
retrograde
retrogression
retrogressive
retrospect
retrospection
retrospective
retroversion
return
returnable
reunion
reunite
revalue
revamp
reveal
revealed
revealingly
revealment
reveille
revel
revelation
reveler
revelry
revenge
revenged
revengeful
revenue
reverberant
reverberate
reverberation

reverberative	revision	rhapsodize
reverberator	revisit	rhapsody
reverberatory	revitalization	rhenium
revere	revitalize	rheostat
revered	revival	rhesus
reverence	revive	rhetoric
reverend	revived	rhetorical
reverent	revivification	rhetorician
reverential	revivify	rheum
reverie	revocable	rheumatic
reversal	revocation	rheumatism
reverse	revoke	rheumatoid
reversibility	revolt	rhinal
reversible	revolted	rhinestone
reversion	revoltingly	rhinitis
reversionary	revolution	rhinocerous
revert	revolutionary	rhinology
reverted	revolutionist	rhodium
revertible	revolutionize	rhomboid
revetment	revolve	rhombus
revictual	revolved	rhubarb
review	revolver	rhyme
reviewed	revulsion	rhythm
reviewer	revulsive	rhythmic
revile	reward	rhythmical
reviled	rewarded	Rialto
revilement	rewardingly	rib
revilingly	rewrite	ribald
revise	rewritten	ribaldry
revised	rhapsodic	ribbon
reviser	rhapsodist	rice

217

rich	rightly	rip
richer	rightness	riparian
riches	rigid	ripe
richest	rigidity	ripely
richly	rigidly	ripen
richness	rigidness	ripened
rickets	rigor	riper
ricochet	rigorous	ripest
riddance	rile	ripple
ridden	riled	ripply
riddle	rill	riprap
ride	rim	rise
rider	rime	risen
riderless	rind	riser
ridge	ring	risibility
ridicule	ringbolt	risk
ridiculed	ringbone	risky
ridiculous	ringed	rite
ridiculously	ringer	ritual
riffraff	ringingly	ritualistic
riffle	ringleader	ritually
riffled	ringlet	rival
rifled	ringlets	rivalry
rifleman	ringmaster	river
rigger	ringside	riverside
right	rink	rivet
righteous	rinse	rivulet
righteously	riot	roach
righteousness	riotous	road
rightful	riotously	roadbed
rightfully	riotousness	roadhouse

roadstead	roguery	roomy
roadster	roguish	roost
roadway	roguishly	rooster
roam	roil	root
roamed	roister	rooted
roamer	roisterer	rooter
roamings	roll	rootlet
roar	rolled	rootlets
roared	roller	rope
roarings	romaine	roquet
roast	Roman	rosaceous
roaster	romance	rosary
rob	Romanesque	rose
robber	romantic	roseate
robbery	romantically	rosette
robin	romanticism	rosewood
robust	romp	rosily
robustly	rompers	rosin
robustness	rondeau	rosiness
rock	roof	roster
rocker	roofer	rostrum
rocket	roofless	rosy
rockweed	rooftree	rot
rocky	rook	Rotarian
rococo	rookery	rotary
rod	room	rotate
rodent	roomed	rotated
rodeo	roomer	rotation
rodman	roomful	rotative
roe	roominess	rotator
rogue	roommate	rotatory

219

rote	roundsman	rubbish
rotenone	roundworm	rubicund
rotogravure	rouse	ruble
rotor	roused	rubric
rotten	rousingly	ruby
rottenness	rout	rucksack
rotund	route	rudder
rotunda	routed	ruddily
rotundity	routed	ruddiness
rouge	routine	ruddy
rough	rover	rude
roughage	rovings	rudely
roughcast	row	rudeness
roughdry	row	ruder
roughen	rowboat	rudest
roughened	rowdy	rudiment
rougher	rowed	rudimental
roughest	rowel	rudimentary
roughhew	rowen	rueful
roughly	rower	ruff
roughneck	rowlock	ruffian
roughness	royal	ruffle
roughrider	royalism	ruffled
roulade	royalist	Rugby
roulette	royally	rugged
round	royalty	ruin
rounder	rub	ruination
roundest	rubber	ruined
roundhouse	rubberize	ruinous
roundly	rubbery	rule
roundness	rubbings	ruled

ruler	rung	rust
rulings	runic	rustic
rum	runner	rusticate
rumble	runt	rustication
ruminant	runway	rusticity
ruminate	rupee	rustily
rumination	rupture	rustiness
ruminative	ruptured	rustle
rummage	rural	rustled
rumor	ruralize	rustler
rumored	rurally	rustlingly
rump	ruse	rusty
rumple	rush	rut
rumpus	rushingly	rutabaga
run	rusk	ruthenium
runabout	russet	ruthless
rune	Russian	rye

S

Sabbatarian	sad	sagittal
Sabbath	sadden	sago
sabbatical	sadder	sahib
saber	saddest	said
sable	saddle	sail
sabotage	saddlebag	sailboat
saccharin	saddler	sailfish
sachem	saddlery	sailings
sachet	sadiron	sailor
sack	sadly	saint
sackcloth	sadness	sainted
sackful	safe	sainthood
sacral	safeguard	saintliness
sacrament	safekeeping	saintly
sacramental	safely	sake
sacred	safeness	salaam
sacredly	safer	salability
sacredness	safest	salable
sacrifice	safety	salacious
sacrificed	saffron	salaciously
sacrificial	sag	salaciousness
sacrilege	saga	salad
sacrilegious	sagacious	salamander
sacristan	sagaciously	salary
sacristy	sagacity	sale
sacrosanct	sagamore	saleratus
sacrum	sage	salesman

salience	salvo	sandman
salient	Samaritan	sandpaper
saliferous	samarium	sandpiper
saline	same	sandstone
saliva	sameness	sandwich
salivate	samite	sandy
salivation	Samoan	sane
sallow	samovar	sanely
sally	sampan	sanguinary
salmon	sample	sanguine
saloon	sampled	sanitarium
salsify	sampler	sanitary
salt	samplings	sanitation
saltcellar	samurai	sanity
salted	sanatorium	Sanskrit
saltpeter	sanatory	sap
salty	sanctification	sapience
salubrious	sanctify	sapient
salubrity	sanctimonious	sapling
salutary	sanctimoniously	saponification
salutation	sanctimoniousness	saponify
salutatorian	sanction	sapper
salutatory	sanctitude	sapphire
salute	sanctity	sapwood
saluted	sanctuary	saraband
salvage	sanctum	Saracen
salvaged	sand	sarcasm
salvation	sandal	sarcastic
salve	sandbag	sarcastically
salve	sandblast	sarcoma
salver	sandiness	sarcophagi

223

sarcophagus	satisfactory	savings
sardine	satisfied	savior
Sardinian	satisfy	savor
sardonic	satisfyingly	savorless
sardonically	satrap	savory
sardonyx	saturate	saw
sarong	saturated	sawdust
sarsaparilla	saturation	sawed
sartorial	Saturday	sawfly
sash	Saturn	sawhorse
sassafras	saturnine	sawmill
sat	satyr	sawn
Satan	sauce	Saxon
satanic	saucepan	say
satchel	saucer	sayings
sateen	saucily	says
satellite	saucy	scab
satiate	saunter	scabbard
satiation	sauntered	scabby
satiety	saunterer	scabies
satin	saurian	scabrous
satinette	sausage	scaffold
satire	sauterne	scald
satiric	savable	scalded
satirical	savage	scale
satirically	savagely	scaled
satirist	savagery	scalene
satirize	savanna	scallion
satirized	savant	scallop
satisfaction	save	scalp
satisfactorily	saved	scalpel

scaly	scarification	schizoid
scamp	scarify	schizophrenia
scamper	scarlatina	scholar
scan	scarlet	scholarly
scandal	scathing	scholarship
scandalization	scathingly	scholastic
scandalize	scatter	scholasticism
scandalized	scattered	scholium
scandalous	scatteringly	school
scandalously	scavenger	schoolbook
Scandinavian	scenario	schoolboy
scandium	scene	schoolhouse
scansion	scenery	schoolmaster
scansorial	scenic	schoolmate
scant	scenical	schoolroom
scantily	scent	schoolwork
scantiness	scented	schoolyard
scantling	scepter	schooner
scanty	sceptered	schottische
scapegoat	schedule	sciatica
scaphoid	scheduled	science
scapula	schematic	scientific
scapular	schematize	scientifically
scar	scheme	scientist
scarab	schemed	scimitar
scarce	schemer	scintillant
scarcely	scherzo	scintillate
scarcity	schism	scintillated
scare	schismatic	scintillation
scared	schismatical	scion
scarf	schist	scissors

225

scleritis	scoundrelly	screen
sclerosis	scour	screened
sclerotic	scoured	screenings
sclerotitis	scourge	screw
sclerotomy	scourged	screwed
scoff	scourings	scribble
scoffed	scout	scribbler
scoffer	scouted	scribe
scoffingly	scow	scrimmage
scold	scowl	scrimp
scolded	scowled	scrip
scoldings	scowlingly	script
scone	scramble	scriptural
scoop	scrap	scripture
scoot	scrapbook	scrivener
scooter	scraper	scrod
scope	scrapings	scrofula
scopolamine	scrapple	scrofulous
scorch	scrappy	scroll
scorcher	scratch	scrollwork
scorchingly	scratchiness	scrub
score	scratchy	scrubbed
scored	scrawl	scrubbings
scorn	scrawled	scrubby
scorned	scrawniness	scrummage
scornful	scrawny	scruple
scornfully	scream	scrupulosity
scorpion	screamed	scrupulous
Scot	screech	scrupulously
Scotch	screechy	scrupulousness
scoundrel	screed	scrutinize

scrutinized	seal	seaward
scrutinizingly	sealed	sebaceous
scrutiny	sealer	secant
scud	sealskin	secede
scudded	seam	secession
scuff	seaman	secessionist
scuffle	seamanship	seclude
scull	seamless	secluded
sculled	seamstress	seclusion
scullery	seamy	second
scullion	seaplane	secondarily
sculpin	seaport	secondary
sculptor	sear	seconded
sculptural	search	seconder
sculpture	searcher	secondhand
sculpturesque	searchingly	secondly
scum	searchlight	secrecy
scupper	seared	secret
scurrility	seascape	secretarial
scurrilous	seashore	secretariat
scurrilously	seasick	secretary
scurry	seasickness	secrete
scurvy	seaside	secreted
scuttle	season	secretion
scuttled	seasonable	secretive
scythe	seasonal	secretively
sea	seasonally	secretly
seaboard	seasoned	secretory
seacoast	seasonings	sect
seafarer	seat	sectarian
seafowl	seated	sectarianism

227

sectary	seducer	segregate
section	seducible	segregated
sectional	seduction	segregation
sectionalism	seductive	seguidilla
sectionalize	seductively	seine
sectionalized	seductiveness	seismic
sectionally	sedulous	seismograph
sector	sedulously	seismology
secular	sedum	seizable
secularism	see	seize
secularize	seed	seizure
secularized	seediness	seldom
secure	seedling	select
secured	seedy	selected
securely	seek	selection
security	seeker	selective
sedan	seem	selectivity
sedate	seemed	selectmen
sedately	seemingly	selector
sedateness	seemliness	selenate
sedative	seemly	selenide
sedentary	seep	selenite
sedge	seepage	selenium
sediment	seersucker	self
sedimentary	seesaw	self-assertion
sedimentation	seethe	self-assured
sedition	seethed	self-colored
seditious	segment	self-command
seditiously	segmental	self-complacency
seditiousness	segmentary	self-complacent
seduce	segmentation	self-conceit

228

self-confidence	self-made	semantic
self-conscious	self-opinionated	semaphore
self-consciousness	self-perception	semblance
self-contained	self-possessed	semester
self-contradiction	self-possession	semiannual
self-contradictory	self-registering	semicircle
self-control	self-reliance	semicircular
self-deceit	self-reliant	semicivilized
self-defense	self-renunciation	semicolon
self-denial	self-reproach	semidetached
self-destruction	self-reproachful	semifinal
self-determination	self-respect	semimonthly
self-determined	self-restraint	seminar
self-educated	self-righteous	seminary
self-esteem	self-righteousness	Seminole
self-evident	self-sacrifice	semiofficial
self-examination	selfsame	semiopaque
self-executing	self-satisfied	semiprecious
self-explaining	self-seeker	Semite
self-explanatory	self-service	Semitic
self-government	self-starter	Semitism
self-help	self-styled	semitone
self-importance	self-sufficiency	semitranslucent
self-induced	self-sufficient	semitransparent
self-indulgence	self-surrender	semiweekly
self-indulgent	self-sustaining	semolina
self-interest	self-winding	sempiternal
selfish	sell	senate
selfishly	sellout	senator
selfishness	Seltzer	senatorial
self-love	selvage	senatorially

senatorship	sensual	separatist
send	sensualism	separatists
sender	sensuality	separative
Seneca	sensually	separator
senescence	sensuous	sepia
senescent	sensuously	sepoy
senile	sensuousness	sepsis
senility	sentence	September
senior	sentenced	septennial
seniority	sententious	septet
senna	sententiously	septic
sennit	sententiousness	septicemia
sensate	sentience	septum
sensation	sentiency	sepulcher
sensational	sentient	sepulchral
sensationalism	sentiently	sepulture
sensationally	sentiment	sequel
sense	sentimental	sequela
senseless	sentimentalism	sequelae
senselessly	sentimentalist	sequence
senselessness	sentimentalists	sequential
sensibility	sentimentality	sequentially
sensible	sentimentally	sequester
sensitive	sentinel	sequestered
sensitively	sentry	sequestrate
sensitiveness	separability	sequestrated
sensitivity	separable	sequestration
sensitization	separate	sequin
sensitize	separated	sequoia
sensitizer	separately	seraglio
sensory	separation	seraph

seraphic	servant	severe
seraphical	serve	severely
seraphim	served	severity
Serbian	server	sew
serenade	service	sewage
serenaded	serviceability	sewed
serenata	serviceable	sewer
serene	serviceably	sewerage
serenely	servile	sewn
sereneness	servility	sextant
serenity	servings	sextet
serf	servitor	sexton
serfdom	servitude	shabbiness
serge	sesame	shabby
sergeant	session	shack
serial	set	shackle
serially	setback	shackled
sericulture	setoff	shade
series	settee	shaded
serif	setter	shadier
serious	settings	shadiest
seriously	settle	shadily
seriousness	settled	shadiness
sermon	settlement	shadings
sermonize	settler	shadow
sermonized	sever	shadowy
serous	severable	shady
serpent	several	shaft
serpentine	severally	shag
serpiginous	severalty	shaggy
serum	severance	shake

231

shaken	shape	sheared
shaker	shapeless	shearings
Shakespearean	shapelessly	shears
shakily	shapelessness	sheathe
shakiness	shapeliness	sheathed
shako	shapely	sheave
shaky	shard	shed
shale	share	sheen
shall	shared	sheep
shallop	sharer	sheepish
shallot	shareholder	sheepishly
shallow	shark	sheepishness
shallowly	sharp	sheepskin
shallowness	sharpen	sheer
sham	sharpened	sheerer
shamble	sharpener	sheerest
shame	sharper	sheet
shamed	sharpest	sheetings
shamefaced	sharply	shelf
shameful	sharpness	shell
shamefully	sharpshooter	shellac
shamefulness	shatter	shellfish
shameless	shattered	shellproof
shamelessly	shave	shelter
shamelessness	shaver	sheltered
shampoo	shavings	shelterless
shamrock	shawl	shelve
shanghai	Shawnee	shelved
shank	she	shepherd
shan't	sheaf	Sheraton
shanty	shear	sherbet

232

sheriff	shipwreck	shortage
sherry	shipwright	shortcake
shibboleth	shipyard	shortchange
shield	shire	shortcomings
shift	shirk	shorten
shiftily	shirker	shorter
shiftiness	shirr	shortest
shiftless	shirred	shorthand
shifty	shirt	shortly
shim	shirtings	shortness
shimmer	shiver	shortsighted
shimmered	shivered	shortstop
shimmery	shoal	shot
shin	shock	should
shine	shockingly	shoulder
shiner	shoddy	shouldered
shingle	shoe	shout
shingled	shoes	shouted
Shinto	shook	shove
shiny	shoot	shovel
ship	shootings	shoveled
shipboard	shop	shovelhead
shipbuilder	shopkeeper	show
shipload	shoplifter	showboat
shipmaster	shopman	showed
shipmate	shopper	shower
shipment	shopworn	showered
shipowner	shore	showily
shipper	shored	showiness
shipshape	shorn	showings
shipworm	short	showman

shown	shudder	sickeningly
showroom	shuddered	sicker
showy	shudderingly	sickest
shrank	shuffle	sickle
shrapnel	shuffled	sickliness
shred	shun	sickly
shrew	shunned	sickness
shrewd	shunt	side
shrewdly	shut	sideboard
shrewdness	shutdown	sidelong
shriek	shutoff	sidepiece
shrift	shutout	sides
shrike	shutter	sidereal
shrill	shuttered	siderite
shrillness	shuttle	sidesaddle
shrilly	shuttled	sidetrack
shrimp	shy	sidewalk
shrine	shyly	sidings
shrink	shyness	sidle
shrinkage	shyster	sidled
shrinkingly	sialagogue	siege
shrive	Siamese	Sienna
shrivel	sibilance	sierra
shriveled	sibilant	siesta
shroud	sibyl	sieve
shrub	sibylline	sift
shrubbery	Sicilian	sifted
shrug	sick	sigh
shrunk	sickbed	sight
shrunken	sicken	sighted
shuck	sickened	sightless

234

sightliness	silicon	simpered
sightly	silicosis	simple
sigmoid	silk	simpler
signal	silken	simplest
signaled	silkiness	simpleton
signalize	silkweed	simplicity
signalized	silkworm	simplification
signally	silky	simplify
signatory	sill	simply
signature	sillabub	simulacrum
signboard	silliness	simulate
signed	silly	simulation
signer	silo	simultaneous
signet	silt	simultaneously
significance	silvan	sin
significant	silver	since
significantly	silversmith	sincere
signification	silverware	sincerely
signify	silvery	sincerity
signpost	simian	sine
silage	similar	sinecure
silence	similarity	sinew
silenced	similarly	sinewy
silencer	simile	sinful
silent	similitude	sing
silently	simmer	singable
silentness	simmered	singe
silex	simony	singer
silhouette	simoom	single
silica	simoon	singled
silicate	simper	singleness

singly	site	skillfully
singular	sitter	skim
singularity	sittings	skimmed
singularly	situated	skimmer
sinister	situation	skimpy
sinistral	sixth	skinflint
sink	sizable	skinny
sinker	size	skip
sinless	sized	skipper
sinlessly	sizes	skirmish
sinned	sizzle	skirmisher
sinner	skate	skirt
sinuosity	skater	skitter
sinuous	skein	skittish
sinus	skeletal	skittishly
sinusitis	skeleton	skittishness
Sioux	skeletonize	skittles
sip	skeptic	skiver
siphon	skeptical	skulk
siphoned	skepticism	skull
sir	sketch	skunk
sire	sketchily	sky
siren	sketchy	skylark
sirloin	skew	skylight
sirocco	skewer	skyrocket
sirup	ski	skyscraper
sister	skid	skyward
sisterhood	skiff	slab
sister-in-law	skill	slack
sisterly	skilled	slacken
sit	skillful	slackened

236

slackness	slayings	slid
slag	sleaziness	slide
slain	sleazy	slier
slake	sled	sliest
slam	sledge	slight
slammed	sleek	slighter
slander	sleekly	slightest
slandered	sleekness	slightingly
slanderer	sleep	slightly
slanderous	sleeper	slightness
slang	sleepily	slim
slangy	sleepiness	slime
slant	sleepless	slimily
slanted	sleeplessness	sliminess
slantingly	sleepy	slimmer
slap	sleet	slimmest
slapdash	sleeve	slimness
slash	sleigh	slimy
slat	sleight	sling
slattern	slender	slink
slatternly	slenderer	slinkiest
slaughter	slenderest	slip
slaughtered	slenderness	slipknot
slaughterer	slept	slippage
slaughterhouse	sleuth	slipper
slave	slew	slipperiness
slavery	slice	slippery
slavish	sliced	slipshod
slaw	slicer	slit
slay	slick	slither
slayer	slicker	sliver

237

slob	slugger	smash
slobber	sluggish	smashup
sloe	sluggishly	smatter
slog	sluggishness	smear
slogan	sluice	smeared
sloop	sluiceway	smell
slop	slum	smelled
sloppy	slumber	smelt
slosh	slumbered	smelter
slot	slumberer	smilax
sloth	slumberous	smile
slothful	slump	smiled
slothfully	slung	smilingly
slothfulness	slur	smirch
slouch	slurred	smirk
slouchily	slush	smite
slouchiness	slushy	smith
slouchy	sly	smithy
slough	slyly	smitten
slough	smack	smock
slovenliness	small	smoke
slovenly	smaller	smokeless
slow	smallest	smoker
slower	smallness	smokestack
slowest	smallpox	smokiest
slowly	smart	smoky
slowness	smarten	smolder
sloyd	smarter	smoldered
sludge	smartest	smooth
slug	smartly	smoothed
sluggard	smartness	smoother

238

smoothest	snarled	snort
smoothly	snatch	snout
smoothness	snath	snow
smote	sneak	snowball
smother	sneaker	snowbound
smothered	sneakiest	snowdrift
smudge	sneaky	snowdrop
smug	sneer	snowfall
smuggle	sneered	snowflake
smuggled	sneeringly	snowiness
smuggler	sneeze	snowplow
smugly	sneezed	snowshed
smugness	sneezeweed	snowshoe
smut	snicker	snowslide
smuttiest	snickered	snowslip
smutty	sniff	snowstorm
snack	sniffle	snowy
snaffle	sniffled	snub
snag	snip	snuff
snail	snipe	snuffer
snake	snob	snuffle
snaky	snobbery	snug
snap	snobbish	snuggery
snapdragon	snobbishly	snuggle
snapper	snobbishness	snuggled
snappish	snood	snugly
snappy	snoop	snugness
snapshot	snoot	so
snare	snooze	soak
snared	snore	soap
snarl	snored	soapiness

239

soapstone	sodden	solicitation
soapy	sodium	solicitor
soar	sofa	solicitous
soared	soft	solicitude
sob	soften	solid
sober	softer	solidarity
soberly	softest	solidification
sobriety	softly	solidify
sobriquet	softness	solidity
soccer	soggy	solidly
sociability	soil	solidness
sociable	soiled	soliloquize
sociably	sojourn	soliloquy
social	sojourned	solitaire
socialism	solace	solitary
socialist	solar	solitude
socialistic	solarium	solo
socialization	solder	soloist
socialize	soldier	solstice
socialized	soldierly	solubility
socially	soldiery	soluble
socialness	sole	solution
society	solecism	solvable
sociological	solely	solve
sociology	solemn	solvency
sock	solemnity	solvent
socket	solemnization	somber
Socratic	solemnize	sombrero
sod	solemnly	some
soda	solenoid	somebody
sodality	solicit	somehow

240

someone	sophistication	soundless
somersault	sophistry	soundly
something	sophomore	soundness
sometime	soporific	soup
somewhat	soprano	sour
somewhere	sorcerer	source
somnambulism	sorcery	soured
somnambulist	sordid	souse
somnolent	sordidness	south
son	sore	southeast
sonata	sorely	southeasterly
song	sorghum	southeastern
songster	sorority	southerly
sonic	sorosis	southern
son-in-law	sorrow	southerner
sonnet	sorrowful	southernmost
sonority	sorrowfully	southward
sonorous	sorry	southwest
soon	sort	southwesterly
sooner	sorted	souvenir
soonest	sorter	sovereign
soot	sortie	sovereignty
soothe	soubrette	Soviet
soothed	sought	sow
soothingly	soul	sow
soothsayer	soulful	soy
sooty	soulless	soya
sop	soullessly	spa
sophism	soullessness	space
sophist	sound	spacious
sophisticate	sounded	spaciously

241

spaciousness	spatter	speckled
spade	spattered	spectacle
spadefish	spatula	spectacular
spaghetti	spatulate	spectacularly
span	spawn	spectator
spandrel	spawned	specter
spangle	speak	spectral
spangled	speaker	spectroscope
spaniel	spear	spectrum
Spanish	speared	speculate
spank	spearfish	speculated
spanked	spearhead	speculates
spankings	special	speculation
spanner	specialist	speculative
spare	specialization	speculator
spared	specialize	speculatory
sparerib	specialized	speculum
sparingly	specially	speech
spark	specialty	speechless
sparkle	specie	speechlessly
sparkled	species	speechlessness
sparklingly	specific	speed
sparrow	specifically	speedboat
sparse	specification	speedily
sparsely	specify	speedometer
sparsity	specimen	speedway
Spartan	specious	speedy
spasm	speciously	spell
spasmodic	speciousness	spellbound
spasmodically	speck	spelled
spastic	speckle	speller

spellings	spinner	splice
spelt	spinneret	splicer
spend	spinster	splint
spendthrift	spinsterhood	splinter
spent	spiny	split
spermaceti	spiral	splurge
spew	spiraled	splutter
sphagnum	spirally	spoil
sphere	spire	spoilage
spherical	spired	spoiled
spheroid	spirit	spoke
sphinx	spirited	spoken
spice	spiritual	spokeshave
spiced	spiritualism	spokesman
spiciness	spiritualist	spoliation
spicy	spirituality	spoliative
spider	spiritualize	spoliator
spidery	spiritually	spondee
spigot	spirituous	sponge
spike	spirochete	sponger
spill	spit	spongy
spilled	spite	sponsor
spillway	spiteful	sponsorship
spin	spittoon	spontaneity
spinach	splash	spontaneous
spinal	spleen	spook
spindle	splendid	spool
spine	splendidly	spoon
spineless	splendor	spoonful
spinet	splendorous	spoor
spinnaker	splenetic	sporadic

spore	springy	squad
sport	sprinkle	squadron
sportive	sprinkled	squalid
sportsman	sprinkler	squalidity
sportsmanship	sprint	squalidly
sporty	sprinter	squall
spot	sprite	squalor
spotless	spritsail	squander
spotlessly	sprocket	square
spotlessness	sprout	squared
spotlight	spruce	squarehead
spotted	sprung	squarely
spotter	spry	squareness
spotty	spud	squash
spouse	spume	squat
spout	spun	squatter
sprain	spunk	squaw
sprained	spunky	squawfish
sprawl	spur	squeak
sprawled	spurred	squeal
spray	spurious	squealed
sprayer	spuriously	squeamish
spread	spurn	squeegee
spreader	spurned	squeeze
spree	spurt	squeezed
sprig	spurted	squelch
sprightliness	sputter	squib
sprightly	sputtered	squid
spring	sputum	squint
springboard	spy	squire
springtime	squab	squirm

244

squirmed	stairway	stannous
squirmings	stake	stanza
squirrel	stalactite	staple
squirt	stalagmite	stapler
stab	stale	star
stability	stalemate	starboard
stabilization	stalk	starch
stabilize	stall	starchy
stabilized	stalled	stare
stabilizer	stallion	stared
stable	stamen	starfish
staccato	stamina	stark
stack	stammer	starless
stadia	stammered	starlight
stadium	stammerer	starling
staff	stamp	starred
stag	stampede	starry
stage	stampeded	start
stagecoach	stampings	started
stagecraft	stanch	starter
stagger	stanchion	startle
staggered	stand	startled
stagnant	standard	starvation
stagnate	standardization	starve
stagnation	standardize	state
staid	standpipe	stated
stain	standpoint	statehood
stained	standstill	statehouse
stainless	stank	stateliness
stair	stannate	stately
staircase	stannic	statement

245

stateroom	steak	stenciled
statesman	steal	stenographer
static	stealth	stenographic
station	stealthily	stenography
stationary	steam	stenosis
stationer	steamboat	stentorian
stationery	steamed	step
statistical	steamer	stepchild
statistically	steampipe	stepdaughter
statistician	steamship	stepladder
statistics	steamy	stepmother
statuary	steatite	steppe
statue	steel	stepped
statuesque	steelwork	stepson
statuette	steep	stereopticon
stature	steeper	stereoscope
status	steepest	stereotype
statute	steeple	sterile
statutory	steeplechase	sterility
stave	steeply	sterilization
stay	steepness	sterilize
stayed	steer	sterilized
stead	steerage	sterilizer
steadfast	steered	sterling
steadfastly	steersman	stern
steadfastness	stein	sterner
steadier	stellar	sternest
steadiest	stem	sternly
steadily	stemmed	sternness
steadiness	stench	sternpost
steady	stencil	sternum

sternutation	stiletto	stipulate
stertorous	still	stipulated
stet	stillborn	stipulates
stethoscope	stillness	stipulation
stevedore	stilly	stir
stew	stilt	stirred
steward	stilted	stirringly
stick	stimulant	stirrings
sticker	stimulate	stirrup
stickful	stimulated	stitch
stickier	stimulates	stoat
stickiest	stimulation	stock
stickiness	stimuli	stockade
stickler	stimulus	stockbroker
stickpin	sting	stockholder
stickweed	stinger	stockily
sticky	stingier	stockiness
stiff	stingiest	stockinet
stiffen	stingily	stockings
stiffened	stinginess	stockman
stiffness	stingy	stocky
stifle	stink	stockyard
stifled	stinker	stogy
stiflingly	stinkpot	stoic
stigma	stinkweed	stoical
stigmas	stint	stoicism
stigmata	stinted	stoke
stigmatic	stipend	stokehold
stigmatism	stipendiary	stoker
stigmatize	stipple	stole
stile	stippled	stolen

247

stolid	stouter	strange
stolidity	stoutest	strangely
stolidly	stouthearted	strangeness
stomach	stoutly	stranger
stone	stoutness	strangest
stoned	stove	strangle
stoneware	stow	strangled
stonework	stowage	strangler
stonily	stowaway	strangles
stoniness	strabismus	strangulate
stony	straddle	strangulated
stood	straddled	strangulation
stool	straggle	strap
stoop	straggled	strata
stop	straggler	stratagem
stopgap	straight	strategic
stoppage	straightedge	strategical
stopped	straighten	strategist
stopper	straightened	strategy
stopple	straightforward	stratification
storage	straightforwardness	stratify
store	straightway	stratum
stored	strain	stratus
storehouse	strained	straw
storeroom	strainer	strawberry
stork	strait	stray
storm	straiten	streak
stormed	straitened	streaky
stormy	strake	stream
story	strand	streamed
stout	stranded	streamer

248

streamlet	strikingly	structure
streamlets	string	struggle
streamline	stringed	struggled
street	stringency	struggler
strength	stringent	strum
strengthen	stringently	strummed
strengthened	stringer	strumpet
strenuous	stringpiece	strung
strenuously	stringy	strut
strenuousness	strip	strutted
stress	stripe	strutter
stretch	stripling	strychnine
stretcher	strive	stub
strew	striven	stubble
strewed	strode	stubborn
strewn	stroke	stubby
striate	stroll	stucco
striated	strolled	stuck
striation	stroller	stud
stricken	strong	student
strict	stronger	studied
strictly	strongest	studio
strictness	stronghold	studious
stricture	strongly	study
stride	strontium	stuff
strident	strop	stuffier
stridently	strophe	stuffiest
stridulous	strove	stuffiness
strife	struck	stuffy
strike	structural	stultification
striker	structurally	stultify

249

stumble	stymie	subjectivity
stump	styptic	subjoin
stun	Styx	subjoined
stunned	suasion	subjugate
stunner	suave	subjugation
stunningly	suavely	subjunctive
stunt	suavity	sublease
stunted	subacute	sublet
stupefacient	subaltern	sublimate
stupefaction	subaqueous	sublimated
stupefy	subarctic	sublimation
stupendous	subcaliber	sublime
stupid	subcellar	sublimest
stupidity	subcommittee	subliminal
stupidly	subconscious	sublimity
stupor	subconsciously	subluxation
sturdily	subconsciousness	submarine
sturdiness	subcontract	submerge
sturdy	subcontractor	submersible
sturgeon	subcutaneous	submersion
stutter	subdeacon	submission
stuttered	subdivide	submissive
stutterer	subdivision	submit
sty	subdue	submitted
style	subeditor	subnormal
stylish	subfamily	suboceanic
stylishness	subgroup	subordinate
stylist	subhead	subordination
stylistic	subject	suborn
stylographic	subjection	subornation
stylus	subjective	suborner

250

subpoena	subterraneous	succotash
subscribe	subtitle	succulence
subscribed	subtle	succulent
subscriber	subtler	succumb
subscription	subtlest	such
subsequent	subtlety	suck
subserve	subtly	sucker
subservience	subtract	suckle
subservient	subtracted	suckled
subside	subtraction	suction
subsidence	subtrahend	sudden
subsidiary	subtreasury	suddenly
subsidize	subtropical	suddenness
subsidy	suburb	sudoriferous
subsist	suburban	sudorific
subsistence	suburbanite	sue
subsists	subvention	sued
subsoil	subversion	suède
substance	subversive	suet
substantial	subvert	suffer
substantially	subway	sufferable
substantiate	succeed	sufferance
substantiation	success	suffered
substantive	successful	sufferer
substitute	successfully	sufferings
substituted	succession	suffice
substitution	successive	sufficiency
substratum	successor	sufficient
substructure	succinct	suffix
subterfuge	succinctly	suffocate
subterranean	succor	suffocation

251

suffragan	sulphate	sunbonnet
suffrage	sulphide	sunburn
suffumigate	sulphite	sunburst
suffuse	sulphur	Sunday
suffusion	sulphuric	sunder
sugar	sulphurous	sundial
sugared	sultan	sundry
sugarplum	sultanate	sunfish
sugary	sultry	sunflower
suggest	sum	sunglass
suggestibility	sumac	sunk
suggestible	summarily	sunken
suggestion	summariness	sunless
suggestive	summarization	sunlight
suggestiveness	summarize	sunlit
suicidal	summary	sunned
suicide	summation	sunniness
suicides	summed	sunny
suit	summer	sunrise
suitability	summerhouse	sunset
suitable	summery	sunshade
suite	summit	sunshine
suitor	summon	sunspot
sulk	summoned	sunstroke
sulkily	sump	sup
sulkiness	sumpter	superable
sulky	sumptuary	superabundant
sullen	sumptuous	superannuate
sullenly	sumptuously	superannuation
sullenness	sumptuousness	superb
sully	sunbeam	supercalender

252

supercalendered	supernumerary	supplier
supercargo	superposition	supply
supercharger	supersaturate	support
supercilious	superscription	supporter
superciliously	supersede	suppose
superciliousness	superseded	supposedly
superdreadnought	supersensitive	supposition
supereminent	superstition	supposititious
supererogation	superstitious	suppository
superficial	superstructure	suppress
superficiality	supervene	suppression
superficially	supervened	suppressive
superfluity	supervise	suprarenal
superfluous	supervised	supremacy
superfluously	supervision	supreme
superfluousness	supervisor	supremely
superheat	supervisory	surbase
superhuman	supineness	surcease
superhumanly	supper	surcharge
superimpose	supplant	surcingle
superimposition	supplanted	surd
superinduce	supple	sure
superintend	supplement	surely
superintendence	supplemental	sureness
superintendency	supplementary	surety
superintendent	suppliant	surf
superior	supplicant	surface
superiority	supplicate	surfeit
superlative	supplicated	surge
supernatural	supplication	surgeon
supernaturally	supplicatory	surgery

253

surgical
surly
surmise
surmised
surmount
surname
surpass
surpassingly
surplice
surplus
surprise
surprised
surprisingly
surrebuttal
surrebutter
surrejoinder
surrender
surreptitious
surrey
surrogate
surround
surrounded
surroundings
surtax
surtout
surveillance
survey
surveyed
surveyor
survival
survive

survivorship
susceptibility
susceptible
suspect
suspend
suspended
suspender
suspense
suspension
suspicion
suspicious
sustain
sustained
sustenance
suture
sutured
svelte
swab
swaddle
swaddled
swag
swage
swagger
swaggered
swain
swallow
swamp
swan
swank
swanky
swarm

swarthy
swastika
sway
swayed
swear
sweat
sweatband
sweater
sweatiness
sweatshop
Swedish
sweep
sweeper
sweepingly
sweepings
sweet
sweetbread
sweetbrier
sweeten
sweetened
sweetheart
sweetish
sweetly
sweetmeat
sweetness
swell
swelled
swellings
swelter
sweltered
swelteringly

swerve	sybarite	symposium
swift	sycamore	symptom
swifter	sycophancy	symptomatic
swiftest	sycophant	synagogue
swiftly	sycophantic	synchronize
swiftness	syllabi	synchronous
swill	syllabic	syncopate
swim	syllabicate	syncopation
swimmingly	syllabication	syncope
swindle	syllabification	syndic
swindled	syllabify	syndicalism
swindler	syllable	syndicate
swine	syllabus	syndrome
swineherd	syllabuses	synod
swing	syllogism	synonym
swipe	syllogistic	synonymous
swirl	sylph	synopsis
swirled	sylvan	synoptic
swish	symbol	syntax
Swiss	symbolic	synthesis
switch	symbolical	synthesize
switchboard	symbolism	synthetic
switchman	symbolist	synthetically
swivel	symbolize	syringe
swollen	symmetrical	system
swoon	symmetry	systematic
swoop	sympathetic	systematize
sword	sympathize	systemic
swordfish	sympathizer	systole
swum	sympathy	systolic
swung	symphony	syzygy

255

T

tabasco
tabernacle
tabes
table
tableau
tablecloth
tablet
tablets
tableware
tabloid
taboo
tabor
tabular
tabulate
tabulation
tabulator
tachometer
tacit
tacitly
taciturn
taciturnity
tack
tackle
tackled
tact
tactful
tactical

tactician
tactics
tactile
tactless
tactlessly
tadpole
taffeta
taffrail
taffy
tag
tagged
tail
tailboard
tailings
tailless
tailor
tailpiece
tailrace
tailstock
taint
tainted
take
takedown
taken
taker
takings
talc

talcum
tale
talebearer
talent
talented
talisman
talk
talkative
talker
tall
taller
tallest
tallish
tallness
tallow
tally
Talmud
talon
tamarack
tamarind
tambourine
tame
tamed
tamer
tamest
tameness
tamper

tampered
tampon
tan
tanager
tandem
tang
tangent
tangential
tangentiality
tangerine
tangible
tangle
tangled
tango
tank
tankage
tankard
tanker
tanner
tannery
tannic
tantalization
tantalize
tantalized
tantalum
Tantalus
tantamount
tantrum
tap
taper
tapered

tapestry
tapeworm
tapioca
tapir
tappet
tar
tarantella
tarantula
tardier
tardiest
tardy
tare
target
tariff
tarlatan
tarnish
tarnished
tarpaulin
tarpon
tarragon
tarred
tarry
tart
tartan
task
taskmaster
Tasmanian
tassel
tasseled
taste
tasted

tasteful
tastefully
tasteless
tastily
tasty
tatter
tattered
tattle
tattled
tattoo
tattooed
taunt
taunted
tauntingly
taut
tautological
tautology
tavern
tawdry
tawny
tax
taxable
taxation
taxed
taxes
taxi
taxicab
taxidermist
taxidermy
taximeter
taxpayer

teach
teachability
teachable
teacher
teacherage
teachings
teacup
teakettle
team
teamster
teamwork
tear
tear
tearful
tearless
tease
teased
teasingly
teaspoon
teaspoonful
technical
technicality
technician
technique
technological
technology
tedious
tediously
tedium
teeter
teetered

teeth
teetotal
teetotaler
telautograph
telecast
telegram
telegraph
telegrapher
telegraphic
telegraphy
telepathic
telepathy
telephone
telephonic
telescope
telescopic
teletype
teleview
televise
television
tell
teller
tellingly
tellings
telltale
tellurium
temerity
temper
temperament
temperamental
temperamentally

temperance
temperate
temperately
temperature
tempest
tempestuous
template
temple
tempo
temporal
temporarily
temporary
temporize
temporized
temporizer
tempt
temptation
tempted
tempter
temptingly
temptress
tenability
tenable
tenacious
tenacity
tenancy
tenant
tenantable
tenanted
tenantless
tenantry

258

tend	tepidity	terror
tended	tercentenary	terrorism
tendency	teredo	terrorist
tender	tergiversate	terroristic
tendered	term	terrorization
tenderer	termagant	terrorize
tenderest	termed	terse
tenderfoot	terminable	terseness
tenderloin	terminal	tertiary
tenderly	terminate	tessellation
tenderness	terminated	test
tendon	termination	testament
tendril	terminology	testamentary
tenement	terminus	testator
tenet	termite	testify
tennis	termless	testimonial
tenon	tern	testimony
tenor	ternary	tests
tense	terrace	tetanus
tensile	terraced	tether
tension	terrain	tetragon
tent	terrapin	tetragonal
tentacle	terrestrial	tetralogy
tentative	terrible	Teutonic
tenterhooks	terribly	text
tenuity	terrier	textbook
tenuous	terrific	textile
tenuously	terrifically	textual
tenure	terrify	textually
tepee	territorial	texture
tepid	territory	thalamic

thalamus	theodolite	thereunto
thalassic	theologian	thereupon
thallium	theological	therewith
than	theologically	therm
thank	theology	thermal
thankful	theoretic	thermion
thankfully	theoretical	thermite
thankfulness	theoretically	thermometer
thankless	theorist	thermometric
thanklessly	theorize	thermometrical
thanksgiving	theorizer	thermostat
that	theory	thesaurus
thatch	theosophic	these
thaw	theosophical	theses
the	theosophist	thesis
theater	theosophy	thew
theatrical	therapeutic	they
theatrically	therapeutical	thick
theatricals	therapy	thicken
theft	there	thickened
their	thereabout	thickener
theirs	thereafter	thicker
theism	thereat	thickest
them	thereby	thicket
theme	therefore	thickly
themselves	therefrom	thickness
then	therein	thief
thence	thereof	thievery
thenceforth	thereon	thievish
thenceforward	thereto	thigh
theocracy	theretofore	thill

thimble	those	thrill
thin	thou	thrillingly
thing	though	throat
things	thought	throatily
think	thoughtful	throatiness
thinkable	thoughtless	throaty
thinker	thoughtlessly	throb
thinly	thoughtlessness	thrombosis
thinner	thousand	thrombus
thinness	thousandfold	throne
thinnest	thrall	throng
third	thrash	throttle
thirst	thrashed	throttled
thirstily	thread	through
thirstiness	threadbare	throughout
thirsty	threadworm	throw
this	threat	thrown
thistle	threaten	thrum
thither	threatened	thrummed
thole	threateningly	thrush
thong	three	thrust
thoracic	threnody	thud
thorax	thresh	thug
thorium	threshold	thulium
thorn	threw	thumb
thorny	thrice	thump
thorough	thrift	thunder
thoroughbred	thriftily	thunderbolt
thoroughfare	thriftless	thundered
thoroughly	thriftlessness	thunderous
thoroughness	thrifty	thundershower

Thursday
thus
thwack
thwart
thy
thyme
thymus
thyroid
thyself
tiara
tibia
tick
ticker
ticket
tickle
tickled
tickler
ticklish
tidal
tide
tidewater
tideway
tidily
tidiness
tidings
tidy
tie
tier
tiffin
tiger
tight

tighten
tightened
tightener
tighter
tightest
tightly
tightrope
tightwad
tile
tiled
till
tiller
tilt
tilted
timber
time
timed
timekeeper
timeless
timeliness
timely
timepiece
timer
timetable
timid
timidity
timidly
timorous
timorously
tin
tinct

tincture
tinctured
tinder
tine
tinge
tinged
tingle
tingled
tinker
tinkle
tinkled
tinned
tinnitus
tinny
tinsel
tinsmith
tint
tinted
tintinnabulation
tinware
tiny
tip
tippet
tipple
tippler
tipsy
tiptoe
tiptop
tirade
tire
tired

tireless	toast	tomato
tirelessly	toasted	tomb
tiresome	tobacco	tomboy
tiresomely	toboggan	tombstone
tiresomeness	toccata	tomorrow
tissue	tocsin	ton
Titan	today	tonal
titanic	toddle	tonality
titaniferous	toddled	tone
titanium	toddy	toneless
tithe	toe	tongs
titillate	toenail	tongue
titillated	toffee	tonic
titillation	toga	tonight
titivate	together	tonnage
titivated	toggle	tonneau
titivation	toil	tonsil
title	toiled	tonsillitis
titled	toiler	tonsorial
titmouse	toilet	tonsure
titrate	toilets	tontine
titration	token	too
titter	told	took
tittered	tolerable	tool
titular	tolerance	tooth
titulary	tolerant	toothache
to	tolerate	toothbrush
toad	tolerated	toothed
toadfish	toleration	toothless
toadstool	toll	toothpick
toady	tomahawk	toothsome

263

top	torque	touchable
topaz	torrent	touchdown
topcoat	torrential	touchily
topiary	torrentially	touchiness
topic	torrid	touchingly
topical	torridity	touchstone
topknot	torsion	touchy
topmast	torso	tough
topmost	tort	toughen
topographer	tortoise	toughened
topographic	tortuously	tougher
topographical	tortuousness	toughest
topography	torture	tour
topple	tortured	toured
toppled	torturer	tourist
topsail	Tory	tourists
toque	toss	tourmaline
torch	tossup	tournament
torchwood	total	tourniquet
tore	totaled	tousle
toreador	totalitarian	tousled
torment	totality	tow
tormented	totalization	towage
tormentingly	totally	toward
tormentor	totem	towards
tornado	totter	towboat
torpedo	tottered	towel
torpid	totteringly	tower
torpidity	tottery	towered
torpidly	toucan	toweringly
torpor	touch	towline

264

town
township
toxic
toxicity
toxicology
toxicosis
toy
trace
traceable
tracer
tracery
trachea
tracheal
trachoma
tracings
track
trackage
trackless
trackman
tract
tractability
tractable
traction
tractive
tractor
trade
traded
trader
tradesman
tradition
traditional

traditionally
traffic
trafficked
tragedian
tragedy
tragic
tragical
tragus
trail
trailed
trailer
train
trained
trainer
trainman
trait
traitor
traitorous
traitorously
trajectory
tram
trammel
trammeled
tramp
trample
trampled
tramway
trance
tranquil
tranquillity
tranquilly

transact
transacted
transaction
transatlantic
transcend
transcendence
transcendency
transcendent
transcendental
transept
transfer
transferable
transference
transferred
transfiguration
transfigure
transfigured
transfix
transform
transformation
transformed
transformer
transfusion
transgress
transgression
transgressor
transient

265

transit
transition
transitional
transitionally
transitive
transitory
translatable
translate
translation
translator
transliterate
translucence
translucent
transmigration
transmissible
transmission
transmit
transmittal
transmitter
transmogrify
transmutable
transmutation
transmute
transmuted
transom
transparency
transparent
transpiration
transpire
transpired
transplant

transplantation
transport
transportation
transported
transposal
transpose
transposed
transposition
transship
transshipment
transubstantiation
transverse
trap
trapdoor
trapeze
trapezoid
trapper
trappings
Trappist
trash
trashy
trauma
traumata
traumatic
travail
travel
traveled
traveler
travelogue
traverse
travesty

trawl
trawler
tray
treacherous
treacherously
treacherousness
treachery
treacle
tread
treadle
treadmill
treason
treasonable
treasure
treasured
treasurer
treasury
treat
treated
treatise
treatment
treaty
treble
tree
trek
trellis
tremble
tremblingly
tremblings
tremendous
tremendously

tremolo	tributary	trinity
tremor	tribute	trinket
tremulous	triceps	trinomial
tremulously	trichinosis	trio
tremulousness	trick	trip
trench	trickery	tripe
trenchancy	trickily	tripthong
trenchant	trickiness	triple
trenchantly	trickle	triplet
trencher	trickled	triplets
trend	trickster	triplex
trepan	tricky	triplicate
trephine	tricot	triplication
trepidation	tricycle	triply
trespass	trident	tripod
trespasser	tried	trippingly
trestle	triennial	trireme
trestlework	trifle	trisect
triad	trifled	triturate
trial	trifler	trituration
triangle	trigger	triumph
triangular	trigonometry	triumphal
triangulate	trill	triumphant
triangulation	trilled	triumvir
tribal	trillion	triumvirate
tribasic	trillium	triune
tribe	trilogy	trivalent
tribesman	trim	trivial
tribulation	trimmed	triviality
tribunal	trimmer	trivially
tribune	trimness	trochaic

267

troche	truckle	trustworthiness
troll	truckled	trustworthy
trolley	truckman	trusty
trombone	truculence	truth
troop	truculent	truthful
troopship	trudge	truthfully
trophy	trudged	truthfulness
tropic	true	try
tropical	trueness	tryst
tropically	truffle	tub
trot	truism	tuba
troth	truly	tube
trotter	trump	tuber
troubadour	trumped	tubercle
trouble	trumpery	tubercular
troublesome	trumpet	tuberculin
troublingly	trumpeter	tuberculosis
troublous	trumpetweed	tuberculous
trough	truncate	tuberose
trounce	truncated	tubular
troupe	truncheon	Tuesday
trousers	trundle	tuft
trousseau	trunk	tug
trout	trunnion	tuition
trowel	truss	tularemia
truancy	trust	tulip
truant	trustee	tulipwood
truce	trusteeship	tulle
truck	trustful	tumble
truckage	trustfully	tumbler
trucked	trustfulness	tumor

268

tumult	turgidly	tutorial
tumultuous	Turk	twain
tumultuously	turkey	twang
tumulus	turmeric	twanged
tun	turmoil	tweak
tuna	turn	tweed
tundra	turnbuckle	tweezers
tune	turncoat	twice
tuned	turned	twiddle
tuneful	turner	twiddled
tuneless	turnings	twig
tuner	turnip	twilight
tungsten	turnkey	twill
tunic	turnout	twin
tunnel	turnover	twinborn
tunneled	turnpike	twine
tunny	turnstile	twined
turban	turpentine	twinge
turbid	turpitude	twinkle
turbidity	turquoise	twinkled
turbidly	turret	twirl
turbinate	turreted	twirled
turbine	turtle	twist
turbot	Tuscan	twistings
turbulence	tusk	twit
turbulent	tussle	twitch
turbulently	tussled	twitted
tureen	tutelage	twitter
turf	tutelary	twittered
turgid	tutor	twitteringly
turgidity	tutored	two

269

twofold	typhoon	typography
twosome	typhous	typothetae
tycoon	typhus	tyrannical
type	typical	tyrannicide
typed	typification	tyrannize
typesetter	typify	tyrannous
typewriter	typist	tyranny
typewritten	typographer	tyrant
typhoid	typographic	tyro

U

ubiquitous	umlaut	unassisted
udder	umpire	unassuming
ugliness	umpired	unattached
ugly	unable	unattainable
ukase	unabridged	unattempted
ukulele	unaccented	unattended
ulcer	unacceptable	unauthenticated
ulcerate	unaccompanied	unauthorized
ulceration	unaccountable	unavailable
ulcerative	unaccustomed	unavoidable
ulcerous	unadjusted	unaware
ulna	unadorned	unbalanced
ulnar	unadulterated	unballasted
ulster	unaffected	unbar
ulterior	unaided	unbecomingly
ultimate	unalloyed	unbeknown
ultimately	unalterable	unbeknownst
ultimatum	un-American	unbelief
ultimo	unamiable	unbelievable
ultramarine	unanimous	unbeliever
ultramodern	unanswerable	unbend
ultraviolet	unappeasable	unbendingly
ululate	unapproachable	unbiased
ululation	unappropriated	unbidden
umber	unarmed	unbind
umbrage	unasked	unblemished
umbrella	unassailable	unblushing

271

unbolted	unclassified	uncontrollable
unborn	uncle	unconventional
unbosom	unclean	uncork
unbound	uncleaned	uncounted
unbounded	unclosed	uncouple
unbowed	unclothed	uncouth
unbreakable	uncoil	uncover
unbridled	uncoiled	uncovered
unbuckle	uncollectible	unction
unbuckled	uncomfortable	unctuous
unbusinesslike	uncomfortably	uncultivated
unbutton	uncommon	uncut
uncage	uncommunicative	undamaged
uncanny	uncompanionable	undamped
unceasingly	uncomplimentary	undaunted
unceremonious	uncompromising	undeceive
unceremoniously	unconcealed	undeceived
uncertain	unconcerned	undecided
uncertainly	unconditional	undecipherable
uncertainty	unconditionally	undeciphered
unchallenged	unconfined	undefended
unchangeable	uncongenial	undefiled
uncharitable	unconquerable	undemonstrative
unchecked	unconquered	undeniable
unchristened	unconscionable	under
unchristian	unconscious	underbid
uncivil	unconsciously	underbrush
uncivilized	unconsciousness	undercharge
unclad	unconsidered	underclothes
unclaimed	unconstitutional	undercurrent
unclasp	uncontradicted	undercut

underdose	understandingly	undiscriminating
underestimate	understate	undisguised
underexpose	understatement	undismayed
undergarment	understood	undisposed
underglaze	understudy	undisputed
undergo	undertake	undistinguishable
undergraduate	undertaken	undisturbed
underground	undertaker	undivided
undergrowth	undertone	undo
underhanded	undertook	undone
underlaid	undertow	undoubted
underlie	undervalue	undress
underline	underwater	undrinkable
underling	underwear	undulant
undermine	underwent	undulate
underneath	underworld	undulation
underpaid	underwrite	undulous
underpass	underwriter	undutiful
underpay	underwritten	undying
underpinning	undeserved	unearned
underproduction	undesigned	unearth
underrate	undesired	unearthly
underscore	undestroyed	uneasiness
undersell	undetermined	uneasy
undershirt	undeveloped	uneatable
undershot	undigested	uneaten
undersigned	undignified	uneducated
undersized	undimmed	unembarrassed
underskirt	undisciplined	unemployment
underslung	undisclosed	unencumbered
understand	undiscovered	unendangered

273

unending
unendorsed
unendurable
unenforceable
unenterprising
unenvied
unequal
unequaled
unequally
unequipped
unequivocal
unerring
unessential
unestimated
unethical
uneven
uneventful
unexampled
unexcelled
unexceptionable
unexpected
unexpectedly
unexpectedness
unfaded
unfair
unfairly
unfairness
unfaithful
unfaithfulness
unfaltering
unfamiliar

unfashionable
unfasten
unfastened
unfavorable
unfeeling
unfeelingly
unfeigned
unfermented
unfettered
unfilled
unfinished
unfit
unflattering
unflinchingly
unfold
unforeseen
unforgettable
unforgivable
unformed
unfortified
unfortunate
unfortunately
unfrequented
unfriendly
unfruitful
unfunded
unfurl
unfurled
unfurnished
ungainly
ungodly

ungovernable
ungracious
ungrammatical
ungrateful
ungratefully
ungratefulness
ungrudgingly
unguarded
unguent
unguided
unhackneyed
unhampered
unhandy
unhanged
unhappiness
unhappy
unhardened
unharness
unhatched
unhealthful
unhealthy
unheard
unheeded
unheedful
unhesitatingly
unhinge
unhitch
unholy
unhonored
unhook
unhoped

274

unhorse	uninterrupted	unlace
unhurt	uninviting	unladylike
unhygienic	union	unlatch
unicorn	unionism	unlaundered
unidentified	unionist	unlearn
unification	unionization	unlearned
uniform	unionize	unleash
uniformed	unionized	unleavened
uniformity	unique	unless
uniformly	uniquely	unlettered
unify	uniqueness	unlicensed
unilateral	unison	unlike
unilluminated	unissued	unlikely
unimaginable	unit	unlimited
unimaginative	Unitarian	unlisted
unimpaired	unitary	unlock
unimpeachable	unite	unlocked
unimportant	united	unlooked
unimpressionable	unity	unlovable
unimproved	universal	unluckily
unincorporated	universality	unlucky
uninformed	universally	unmake
uninhabitable	universe	unmanageable
uninhabited	university	unmanly
uninitiated	unjustifiable	unmannerly
uninjured	unkind	unmarried
uninstructed	unkindliness	unmask
unintelligent	unknightly	unmatched
unintelligible	unknowable	unmentionable
unintentional	unknowingly	unmerciful
unintentionally	unknown	unmercifully

unmindful
unmistakable
unmixed
unmolested
unmounted
unnamed
unnatural
unnecessary
unnerve
unnumbered
unobjectionable
unobservant
unobserved
unobtainable
unoccupied
unopened
unopposed
unorganized
unpack
unpaid
unpalatable
unparalleled
unpardonable
unpardoned
unparliamentary
unpaved
unperturbed
unpleasant
unplowed
unpolished
unpolluted

unpopular
unpracticed
unprecedented
unprejudiced
unpremeditated
unprepared
unpreparedness
unprepossessing
unpretentious
unprincipled
unprofessional
unprogressive
unpromising
unproved
unpublished
unpunctual
unqualified
unquestionable
unquestionably
unquestioned
unreasonable
unreasonably
unrebuked
unrecognizable
unrecognized
unreconciled
unredeemed
unrelated
unremitting
unremunerative
unrepaired

unrepentant
unreproved
unrequited
unreserved
unreservedly
unresisting
unrestrained
unrestricted
unrewarded
unrighteous
unripe
unrivaled
unroll
unruffled
unruly
unsaddle
unsafe
unsaid
unsalable
unsanctified
unsatisfactory
unsatisfied
unsavory
unscrew
unscrewed
unscrupulous
unseasonable
unseasoned
unseemly
unseen
unselfish

unselfishly	unsubstantiated	untried
unsettle	unsuccessful	untroubled
unsettled	unsuitable	untrue
unshakable	unsung	untruth
unshaven	unsure	untruthful
unsheathe	unsuspected	untutored
unsheltered	unsweetened	untwine
unship	unswerving	untwist
unshorn	unsympathetic	unusable
unsightly	unsystematic	unused
unsigned	untangle	unusual
unskilled	untangled	unusually
unskillful	untainted	unutterable
unsmirched	unteachable	unuttered
unsnarl	untechnical	unvalued
unsociable	untenanted	unvarnished
unsoiled	untested	unvarying
unsoldierly	unthinkable	unveil
unsolicited	unthinking	unversed
unsophisticated	unthinkingly	unwarrantable
unsought	untidily	unwarranted
unsound	untidy	unwary
unspeakable	untie	unwarily
unspoken	until	unwashed
unsportsmanlike	untiringly	unwaveringly
unstable	unto	unwearied
unstained	untold	unwelcome
unsteadily	untouched	unwell
unsteady	untoward	unwholesome
unstrung	untracked	unwieldy
unsubstantial	untranslatable	unwilling

unwillingly	uprising	usefulness
unwillingness	uproar	useless
unwind	uproarious	uselessly
unwise	uproot	uselessness
unwittingly	upset	user
unwonted	upshot	uses
unworkable	upside	usher
unworldly	upstairs	usual
unworthy	upstart	usually
unwrap	uptake	usufruct
unwreathe	uptown	usurer
unwritten	upturn	usurious
up	upturned	usurp
upas	upward	usurper
upbraid	uranium	usury
upgrowth	urban	utensil
upheaval	urbane	utilitarian
upheld	urbanely	utilitarianism
uphill	urbanity	utilities
uphold	urchin	utility
upholder	urge	utilizable
upholster	urged	utilization
upholsterer	urgency	utilize
upholstery	urgent	utilized
upkeep	urgently	utmost
uplift	urn	Utopia
upmost	usable	Utopian
upon	usage	utter
upper	use	utterance
uppermost	useful	uttered
upright	usefully	utterly

V

vacancy	valedictory	vandalism
vacant	valence	vane
vacate	valentine	vanguard
vacation	valerian	vanilla
vacationist	valet	vanish
vaccinate	valiant	vanity
vaccination	valid	vanquish
vaccine	validate	vantage
vacillate	validated	vapid
vacillatingly	validation	vapidly
vacillation	validity	vapor
vacuity	validly	vaporization
vacuous	valise	vaporize
vacuum	valley	vaporized
vagabond	valor	vaporizer
vagary	valorous	vaporous
vagrancy	valuable	variability
vagrant	valuation	variable
vague	value	variance
vagus	valued	variant
vain	valueless	variation
vainglorious	valve	varicose
vainglory	valvular	varicosity
vainly	valvulitis	varied
vainness	vampire	variegate
valance	vanadium	variegation
valedictorian	vandal	variety

variola	vehicular	venomously
various	veil	ventilate
variously	veiled	ventilation
varnish	vein	ventilator
vary	veined	ventral
vascular	veinlet	ventricle
vase	vellum	ventricular
vaseline	velocipede	venture
vassal	velocity	ventured
vassalage	velure	venturesome
vast	velvet	venue
vat	velveteen	veracious
Vatican	velvety	veracity
vaudeville	venal	veranda
vault	venality	verb
vaulted	vend	verbal
vector	vendee	verbalization
vedette	vender	verbalize
veer	vendible	verbalized
veered	vendor	verbally
vegetable	veneer	verbatim
vegetarian	venerable	verbiage
vegetarianism	venerate	verbose
vegetate	venerated	verbosity
vegetated	veneration	verdant
vegetation	vengeance	verdict
vegetative	vengeful	verdigris
vehemence	venial	verdure
vehement	venially	verge
vehemently	venison	verged
vehicle	venom	verification

verify	vertigo	vibrated
verily	verve	vibration
verisimilitude	very	vibrator
veritable	vesicle	vibratory
veritably	vesper	vicar
verity	vessel	vicarage
vermicelli	vest	vicarious
vermicide	vestal	vicariously
vermiform	vested	vice
vermifuge	vestibular	viceregal
vermilion	vestibule	viceroy
vermin	vestige	vicinity
verminous	vestigial	vicious
vernacular	vestment	viciously
vernal	vestry	vicissitude
vernier	veteran	victim
versatile	veterinarian	victimize
versatility	veterinary	victimized
verse	veto	victor
versification	vex	Victorian
versifier	vexation	victorious
versify	vexatious	victoriously
version	vexed	victory
verso	viability	victual
versus	viable	victualed
vertebra	viaduct	video
vertebrae	vial	vie
vertebrate	viand	vied
vertex	vibrancy	view
vertical	vibrant	viewed
vertically	vibrate	vigil

vigilance	violator	viscidity
vigilant	violence	viscose
vigilantly	violent	viscosity
vignette	violently	viscount
vigor	violet	viscous
vigorous	violets	vise
vigorously	violin	visibility
vile	violinist	visible
viler	viper	vision
vilest	virago	visionary
vilification	vireo	visit
vilify	virgin	visitation
villa	virginal	visited
village	virginity	visitor
villager	virile	vista
vinaigrette	virility	visual
vinculum	virtual	visualization
vindicable	virtually	visualize
vindicate	virtue	visualized
vindication	virtuosity	visually
vindictive	virtuoso	vital
vine	virtuous	vitality
vinegar	virulence	vitalize
vineyard	virulency	vitalized
vintage	virulent	vitally
vinylite	virus	vitamin
viol	visa	vitiate
violate	visage	vitiated
violated	viscera	vitiation
violation	visceral	vitreous
violative	viscid	vitrification

282

vitrify	voided	vomited
vitriol	volatile	vomitory
vituperate	volatility	voodoo
vituperation	volatilization	voracious
vituperative	volatilize	voracity
vivacious	volcanic	vortex
vivaciously	volcano	vortical
vivacity	volition	votary
vivid	volitional	vote
vividly	volley	voter
vivisection	volt	votive
vixen	voltage	vouch
vocabulary	voltameter	vouched
vocal	voltammeter	voucher
vocalism	voltmeter	vouchsafe
vocalist	volubility	vow
vocalization	voluble	vowed
vocalize	volubly	vowel
vocalized	volume	voyage
vocally	volumetric	vulcanization
vocation	voluminous	vulcanize
vocationally	voluntarily	vulgar
vocative	voluntary	vulgarian
vociferous	volunteer	vulgarism
vodka	voluptuary	vulgarity
vogue	voluptuous	vulgarize
voice	voluptuously	vulgarized
voiced	volute	vulgarly
voiceless	volvulus	vulnerability
void	vomica	vulnerable
voidable	vomit	vulture

W

wad	waitress	wandered
waddle	waive	wanderer
wade	waiver	wane
waded	wake	waned
wader	wakeful	wangle
wafer	wakefully	want
waffle	wakefulness	wanted
waft	waken	war
wag	wale	warble
wage	walk	warbler
waged	walker	ward
wager	walkout	warded
wagered	walkover	warden
waggle	wall	warder
waggled	walled	wardrobe
wagon	wallet	wardroom
waif	wallets	warehouse
wail	wallflower	warfare
wailed	wallow	warily
wailings	wallpaper	wariness
wainscot	walnut	warlike
waist	walrus	warm
waistband	waltz	warmed
waistline	wampum	warmly
wait	wan	warmth
waited	wand	warn
waiter	wander	warned

284

warningly	watchcase	waveringly
warp	watchdog	waviness
warrant	watchful	wavy
warranted	watchfully	wax
warrantor	watchfulness	waxen
warranty	watchmaker	waxiness
warren	watchman	waxwing
warship	watchtower	waxy
wart	watchword	way
wary	water	waybill
was	watered	wayfarer
wash	waterfall	waylaid
washable	waterfowl	waylay
washcloth	waterlogged	wayside
washer	Waterloo	wayward
washout	watermark	waywardness
washroom	waterproof	we
washstand	watershed	weak
washwoman	waterside	weaken
wasp	waterspout	weakened
waspish	waterway	weaker
wassail	waterworks	weakest
wastage	watery	weakling
waste	watt	weakly
wastebasket	wattage	weakness
wasted	wattle	wealth
wasteful	wattled	wealthier
wastefully	wattmeter	wealthiest
wastefulness	wave	wealthy
wastrel	waver	weapon
watch	wavered	wear

wearable	weigh	whack
wearer	weighings	whale
wearily	weight	whaleback
weariness	weighty	whalebone
wearings	weir	whaler
weary	weird	wharf
weasel	weirdly	wharfage
weather	weirdness	wharfinger
weatherboard	welcome	what
weathercock	welcomed	whatever
weathered	weld	whatnot
weatherproof	welded	whatsoever
weave	welfare	wheat
weaver	well	wheaten
web	welt	wheatworm
webbing	welter	wheedle
wed	weltered	wheedled
wedded	wen	wheel
wedding	wench	wheelbarrow
wedge	wend	wheeled
wedged	wended	wheelwright
wedlock	went	wheeze
Wednesday	wept	whelk
weed	were	whelp
weedy	west	when
week	westerly	whence
weekday	western	whenever
weekly	westerner	whensoever
weep	westward	where
weevil	wet	whereabouts
weft	wetness	whereas

286

whereat	whip	whittle
whereby	whipcord	whittled
wherefore	whippet	who
wherefrom	whipstitch	whoever
wherein	whipstock	whole
whereof	whipworm	wholehearted
whereon	whir	wholesale
wheresoever	whirl	wholesaler
whereupon	whirled	wholesome
wherever	whirligig	wholesomely
wherewith	whirlpool	wholly
wherewithal	whirlwind	whoop
wherry	whisk	whose
whet	whisker	whosoever
whetted	whisky	why
whether	whisper	wick
which	whispered	wicked
whichever	whisperer	wickedness
whichsoever	whist	wicker
whiff	whistle	wickerwork
Whig	whistled	wicket
while	white	wide
whilom	whitecap	widen
whim	whitefish	wider
whimper	whiten	widespread
whimpered	whiteness	widest
whimsey	whitewash	widow
whimsical	whitewings	widowed
whimsically	whitewood	widower
whine	whither	widowhood
whined	whitlow	width

wield	windlass	wise
wife	windmill	wiseacre
wig	window	wisely
wiggle	windowpane	wiser
wiggled	windpipe	wisest
wigwag	windrow	wish
wigwam	windstorm	wished
wild	windward	wishful
wilderness	windy	wishfully
wildfire	wine	wisp
wildness	wineglass	wistful
wile	wing	wistfully
will	winged	wistfulness
willed	wingless	wit
willful	wink	witch
willfully	winked	witchcraft
willfulness	winkle	witchery
willingly	winner	with
willingness	winningly	withal
willow	winnings	withdraw
wily	winnow	withdrawal
win	winsome	withdrew
wince	winter	wither
winch	wipe	withered
wind	wiper	witheringly
windage	wire	withhold
windbreak	wired	within
windfall	wireless	without
windily	wirepulling	withstand
windings	wireworm	witless
windjammer	wisdom	witness

288

witticism
wittingly
witty
wives
wizard
wizardly
wizardry
wizened
woe
woebegone
woeful
woefully
wolf
wolfhound
wolfish
wolverene
wolves
woman
womanhood
womankind
womanlike
womanliness
womanly
women
won
wonder
wonderful
wonderfully
wonderingly
wonderland
wonderment
wonderwork
wondrous
wondrously
won't
wont
woo
wood
woodchuck
wooded
wooden
woodland
woodman
woodpecker
woodsman
woodwork
woodworm
wooer
woof
wool
woolen
wooliness
woolly
word
wordiness
wordy
work
workable
worked
worker
workhouse
workings
workman
workmanship
workmen
workshop
workwoman
workwomen
world
worldliness
worldly
worm
wormwood
wormy
worn
worried
worrier
worriment
worrisome
worry
worse
worship
worshiped
worshiper
worshipful
worst
worsted
worsted
worth
worthily
worthiness
worthless
worthy

would	wrecker	writ
wound	wren	write
wound	wrench	writer
wove	wrest	writhe
woven	wrestle	writings
wrack	wrestled	written
wraith	wrestler	wrong
wrangle	wretch	wrongful
wrangled	wretchedly	wrongfully
wrap	wretchedness	wrongheaded
wrapper	wriggle	wrongly
wrappings	wriggled	wrongness
wrath	wring	wrote
wrathful	wringer	wroth
wrathfully	wrinkle	wrought
wreath	wrinkled	wrung
wreck	wrist	wry
wreckage	wristlet	wryneck

X Y Z

- xenon
- xeroderma
- xerosis
- X-ray
- xylophone
- xyster

- yacht
- yachtsman
- yak
- Yale
- yam
- yank
- Yankee
- yard
- yardage
- yardarm
- yardstick
- yarn
- yarrow
- yaw
- yawl
- yawn
- ye
- yea
- year
- yearbook

- yearling
- yearly
- yearn
- yearningly
- yearnings
- yeast
- yeasty
- yell
- yelled
- yellow
- yelp
- yeoman
- yeomanry
- yes
- yesterday
- yet
- yew
- yield
- yielded
- yieldingly
- yodel
- yoga
- yolk
- yon
- yonder
- yore
- you

- young
- younger
- youngest
- youngish
- youngster
- your
- yourself
- yourselves
- youthful
- youthfully
- youthfulness
- ytterbium
- yttrium
- yucca
- yule
- yuletide

- zany
- zeal
- zealot
- zealotry
- zealously
- zebra
- zebu
- zenith
- zephyr
- Zeppelin

zero	Zionism	zone
zest	Zionist	zoo
zigzag	zipper	zoological
zinc	zirconium	Zulu
Zion	zodiac	zymology

PART TWO

PERSONAL AND GEOGRAPHICAL NAMES

Part Two consists of 2,604 entries of personal and geographical names divided approximately as follows:

1,600 geographical names. The largest group of names consists of the names of American cities and towns that are likely to be encountered in business dictation. The names of the American states and territories are given. A relatively small group of foreign geographical names is given — the foreign countries and cities that are most likely to occur in American business dictation. The lists are not intended to be complete or exhaustive. The attempt has been made, however, to include the geographical names that occur most frequently in ordinary business dictation.

350 surnames. This small group of last names represents the commonest American last names that are likely to be used in business dictation. There are tens of thousands of surnames in this country, and no attempt can be made to present a complete list.

350 first names of women. This list contains the more frequently used feminine first names.

350 first names of men. This list contains the more frequently used masculine first names.

The four groups of names listed above are combined in one alphabetical list in Part Two.

With the exception of the states and of a few of the largest cities, the geographical names are written very fully. This is done with the understanding that the writer will use these full outlines for the names that occur only occasionally in the dictation. When some name occurs more frequently in the dictation, an abbreviated form will be used.

The shorthand writer in Oregon would ordinarily have little occasion to use the outline for *Corpus Christi*. The Texan shorthand writer might use it so frequently that he would abbreviate it to *kk*.

In order to keep the list in Part Two as short and at the same time as useful as possible the names of many cities and towns are omitted. This is possible because many American city and town names are composed of nouns and adjectives that appear in Part One — such names as *White River Junction* or *Egg Harbor City*.

Many cities and towns form their names by adding to the name of another town a word like *Beach, Grove, Hill, City, Park,* or *Spring*. In most cases such names have been omitted as they would cause no shorthand writing difficulty.

PERSONAL AND GEOGRAPHICAL NAMES

Aaron	Alabama	Alliance
Abbott	Alameda	Allison
Abel	Alamosa	Alma
Aberdeen	Alan	Alonso
Abigail	Alaska	Alpena
Abilene	Albania	Alphonsine
Abington	Albany	Alphonso
Abner	Albert	Althea
Abraham	Alberta	Alton
Abram	Albia	Altoona
Ada	Albion	Altus
Adam	Albuquerque	Alva
Adams	Alcoa	Alvin
Adelaide	Alexander	Amanda
Adelbert	Alexandra	Amarillo
Adler	Alexandria	Ambridge
Adolph	Alexis	Ambrose
Adrian	Alfred	Amelia
Adrienne	Algeria	Americus
Afghanistan	Algernon	Ames
Africa	Alhambra	Amesbury
Agatha	Alice	Amherst
Agnes	Alicia	Amityville
Aiken	Aliquippa	Amos
Aileen	Allan	Amsterdam
Ainsworth	Allen	Amy
Akron	Allentown	Anaconda

Anacortes	Arcadia	Attleboro
Anaheim	Archer	Aubrey
Anastasia	Archibald	Auckland
Andalusia	Ardmore	Audry
Anderson	Argentina	Audubon
Andover	Arizona	Augusta
Andrews	Arkadelphia	Augustin
Angela	Arkansas	Aurelia
Angelica	Arline	Aurelius
Angora	Arlington	Aurora
Angus	Armstrong	Austin
Anita	Arnold	Australia
Ann	Arthur	Austria
Anna	Asa	Avalon
Annabel	Asbury Park	Avery
Annapolis	Asheboro	Avis
Ann Arbor	Asheville	Ayres
Annette	Ashland	Azusa
Anniston	Ashley	Bacon
Anoka	Ashtabula	Bailey
Anselm	Astoria	Bainbridge
Ansonia	Asunción	Baird
Anthony	Atchison	Baker
Antigo	Athelstan	Bakersfield
Antioch	Athena	Baldwin
Antoinette	Athens	Ballard
Antonia	Athol	Baltimore
Antwerp	Atkinson	Bangkok
Appleton	Atlanta	Bangor
Arabella	Atlantic	Baptist
Arabia	Atlantic City	Baptista

296

Baraboo	Beacon	Benedicta
Barbara	Beale	Bender
Barberton	Beardstown	Benjamin
Barcelona	Beatrice	Bennett
Barlow	Beaumont	Bennington
Barnabas	Beaver	Benson
Barnaby	Beaver Dam	Bentley
Barnard	Beaver Falls	Benton
Barnesville	Becker	Benton Harbor
Barnett	Beckley	Berea
Barnstable	Bedford	Bergenfield
Barranquilla	Beecher	Berkeley
Bartholomew	Belfast	Berlin
Barre	Belgium	Bernard
Barrett	Belinda	Bernstein
Barrington	Bell	Bertha
Bartlesville	Bella	Bertram
Bartlett	Bellaire	Bertrand
Bartow	Belle	Berwick
Basil	Bellefontaine	Berwyn
Bastrop	Bellefonte	Beryl
Batavia	Belleville	Bessemer
Batesville	Bellevue	Bessie
Bath	Bellingham	Bethlehem
Baton Rouge	Bellwood	Beulah
Battle Creek	Belmont	Beverly
Bauer	Beloit	Bicknell
Baxter	Belvedere	Biddeford
Bayard	Bemidji	Big Spring
Bay City	Bend	Billings
Bayonne	Benedict	Biloxi

Binghamton	Boonville	Brian
Birmingham	Bordeaux	Bridgeport
Bisbee	Boris	Bridget
Bishop	Boston	Bridgeton
Bismarck	Bosworth	Bridgewater
Bissell	Boulder	Briggs
Blackstone	Bound Brook	Brigham
Blackwell	Bowen	Brisbane
Blair	Bowling Green	Bristol
Blairsville	Bowman	Bristow
Blake	Boyd	Brockton
Blakely	Boyle	Bronxville
Blanchard	Bozeman	Brookfield
Blanche	Brackenridge	Brookhaven
Bliss	Braddock	Brookings
Bloomfield	Bradenton	Brown
Bloomington	Bradford	Brownsville
Bloomsburg	Bradley	Brownwood
Bluefield	Brady	Bruce
Blue Island	Brainerd	Bruno
Bluffton	Braintree	Brunswick
Blytheville	Brattleboro	Brussels
Bogalusa	Brawley	Bryan
Bogota	Brazil	Bryant
Boise	Bremen	Bucharest
Bolivia	Bremerton	Bucyrus
Bombay	Brenham	Budapest
Bonham	Brennan	Buenos Aires
Boniface	Brentwood	Buffalo
Boone	Brewer	Bulgaria
Boonton	Brewster	Burbank

Burke	Camilla	Cartersville
Burley	Campbell	Carthage
Burlingame	Campeche	Casper
Burlington	Canada	Catharine
Burma	Canal Zone	Cathleen
Burns	Canfield	Catskill
Burrillville	Cannon	Cecelia
Burroughs	Canon City	Cecil
Burton	Canonsburg	Cedar Falls
Butler	Canton	Cedarhurst
Butte	Cape Girardeau	Cedar Rapids
Byron	Cape Town	Cedartown
Cable	Caracas	Cedric
Cadillac	Carbondale	Celeste
Cadwallader	Carey	Celestine
Caesar	Carlisle	Celia
Cairo	Carlotta	Centerville
Calais	Carlsbad	Central Falls
Calcutta	Carlson	Centralia
Caldwell	Carlstadt	Ceylon
Caleb	Carlton	Chalmers
Calexico	Carmel	Chambersburg
Calgary	Carmen	Champaign
Calhoun	Carnegie	Chandler
California	Carol	Chanute
Callahan	Carpenter	Chapman
Calumet City	Carroll	Chariton
Calvin	Carrollton	Charleroi
Cambridge	Carson	Charles
Camden	Carter	Charleston
Cameron	Carteret	Charlotte

299

Charlottesville	Cicely	Clifton Forge
Chase	Cicero	Clinton
Chattanooga	Cincinnati	Cloquet
Chauncy	Circleville	Clotilda
Cheboygan	Clairton	Clovis
Chelsea	Clara	Coaldale
Cheltenham	Clare	Coatesville
Cherbourg	Claremont	Cobb
Cherokee	Clarence	Coddington
Chester	Claribel	Coeur d'Alene
Cheviot	Clarice	Coffeyville
Cheyenne	Clarinda	Cohen
Chicago	Clark	Cohoes
Chickasha	Clarksburg	Colby
Chico	Clarksdale	Coldwater
Chicopee	Clarksville	Coleman
Chihuahua	Claudia	College Park
Childress	Claudius	Collier
Childs	Claudine	Collingdale
Chile	Clayton	Collingswood
Chillicothe	Clearfield	Collins
China	Clearwater	Collinsville
Chippewa Falls	Cleary	Cologne
Chisholm	Cleburne	Colombia
Christabel	Clement	Colorado
Christchurch	Clementina	Colorado Springs
Christian	Clementine	Colton
Christina	Cleveland	Columbia
Christine	Clifford	Columbia Heights
Christopher	Cliffside Park	Columbus
Chula Vista	Clifton	Compton

300

Comstock	Corinna	Cudahy
Concord	Corinth	Culbertson
Concordia	Cork	Cullman
Condon	Cornelia	Culver City
Cone	Cornelius	Cumberland
Conklin	Corning	Cummings
Conley	Corona	Cummins
Connecticut	Coronado	Curtis
Connellsville	Corpus Christi	Cushing
Connelly	Corry	Cuthbert
Connersville	Corsicana	Cutler
Connolly	Cortland	Cynthia
Connor	Corvallis	Cyril
Conrad	Corwin	Cyrus
Conshohocken	Coshocton	Czechoslovakia
Constance	Costa Rica	Dagmar
Constant	Council Bluffs	Dallas
Constantine	Covington	Dalton
Constantinople	Crafton	Daly
Conway	Craig	Dan
Cook	Crandall	Danbury
Cooley	Cranford	Daniel
Coolidge	Cranston	Daphne
Cooper	Crawford	Davenport
Copenhagen	Crawfordsville	Danville
Cora	Creston	Darby
Coral Gables	Crispin	Darlington
Coraopolis	Cromwell	Dartmouth
Corbin	Crookston	David
Cordele	Crowley	Davidson
Cordelia	Cuba	Davis

301

Dawson	Des Moines	Dover
Dayton	De Soto	Dowagiac
Daytona Beach	Detroit	Downers Grove
Dean	Devils Lake	Doyle
Dearborn	Dewey	Dresden
Deborah	Dexter	Driscoll
Decatur	Diana	Drusilla
Decker	Dick	Dublin
Decorah	Dickinson	Du Bois
Dedham	Dickson City	Dubuque
Deerfield	Dillon	Dudley
Defiance	Dinah	Duffy
De Kalb	District of Columbia	Dulcie
De Land	Dix	Duluth
Delaware	Dixon	Dumont
Delhi	Dobbs Ferry	Dunbar
Delia	Dodge City	Duncan
Della	Dolores	Dunn
Delphine	Dominic	Dunellen
Delphos	Dominican Republic	Dunkirk
Del Rio	Donald	Dunmore
Demetrius	Donora	Duquesne
Denise	Donovan	Durango
Denison	Dora	Durant
Denmark	Dorcas	Durham
Dennison	Doris	Duryea
Denton	Dormont	Dwight
Denver	Dorothea	Dyersburg
De Pere	Dorothy	Eagle Pass
Depew	Dougherty	Earl
Derby	Douglas	Easley

East Aurora	Effingham	Eloise
East Chicago	Egan	El Paso
Easthampton	Egbert	El Reno
East Hartford	Egypt	Elsa
East Lansing	Eileen	El Salvador
Eastman	Eire	Elsie
East Moline	Elaine	Elspeth
Easton	Elbert	Elton
East Orange	Elberton	Elvira
East Peoria	Eldred	Elwood
East Pittsburgh	El Centro	Ely
East Point	El Cerrito	Elyria
East Providence	Eleanor	Emery
East Rochester	Electra	Emil
East Rutherford	Elgin	Emily
East Stroudsburg	Elihu	Emma
Eau Claire	Elijah	Emmanuel
Ebenezer	Elisha	Emporia
Ecuador	Elizabeth	Endicott
Edgar	Elizabethton	England
Edina	Elk City	Englewood
Edinburgh	Elkhart	Enid
Edith	Elkins	Ennis
Edmonton	Ellen	Enos
Edmund	Ellensburg	Enrico
Edna	Elliott	Enright
Edward	Ellsworth	Ephraim
Edwardsville	Ellwood City	Ephrata
Edwin	Elmer	Erasmus
Edwina	Elmhurst	Erastus
Effie	Elmira	Eric

Erie	Evelina	Fitchburg
Erma	Evelyn	Fitzgerald
Ernest	Everard	Flagstaff
Ernestine	Everett	Flat River
Erwin	Exeter	Flavia
Escanaba	Ezra	Fleming
Estella	Fairbanks	Flint
Esther	Fairbury	Flora
Estherville	Fairfield	Florence
Esthonia	Fairhaven	Florida
Ethan	Fairlawn	Floyd
Ethel	Fairmont	Flynn
Ethiopia	Fairview	Foley
Etna	Faith	Fond du Lac
Etta	Fall River	Ford
Euclid	Falls City	Ford City
Eudora	Fargo	Forest City
Eugene	Farrell	Forest Park
Eugenia	Fayetteville	Forest Hills
Eulalia	Feldman	Fort Atkinson
Eunice	Felix	Fort Collins
Euphemia	Ferdinand	Fort Dodge
Eureka	Fergus Falls	Fort Lauderdale
Europe	Ferguson	Fort Lee
Eustace	Ferndale	Fort Madison
Eva	Fidelia	Fort Myers
Evangeline	Field	Fort Pierce
Evanston	Findlay	Fort Scott
Evansville	Finland	Fort Smith
Eve	Finley	Fort Thomas
Eveleth	Fisher	Fort Wayne

Fort Worth	Gaffney	Gifford
Foster	Gail	Gilbert
Fostoria	Gainesville	Girard
Fox	Galesburg	Gladys
Framingham	Galion	Glasgow
France	Gallagher	Glassport
Frances	Gallup	Gleason
Francis	Galveston	Glencoe
Frankfort	Garden City	Glen Cove
Franklin	Gardiner	Glendale
Fraser	Gardner	Glenn
Frederic	Garfield	Glenna
Frederica	Garret	Glen Ridge
Fredericksburg	Gary	Glen Rock
Fredericton	Gasper	Glens Falls
Freehold	Gastonia	Globe
Freeland	Geneva	Gloria
Freeman	Genevieve	Gloucester
Freeport	Genoa	Gloversville
Fremont	Geoffrey	Goddard
French	George	Godfrey
Fredonia	Georgetown	Goldberg
Fresno	Georgia	Goldsboro
Frieda	Gerald	Goodwin
Frostburg	Geraldine	Gordon
Fuller	Gerard	Goshen
Fullerton	Germany	Gould
Fulton	Gertrude	Grace
Gabriel	Gettysburg	Grafton
Gabriella	Gibson	Graham
Gadsden	Gideon	Grand Forks

305

Grand Haven	Grosse Pointe	Harding
Grand Island	Grove City	Harlan
Grand Junction	Grover	Harley
Grand Rapids	Guadalajara	Harold
Grant	Guam	Harper
Grants Pass	Guatemala	Harriet
Graves	Gulfport	Harriman
Gray	Gustavus	Harrington
Great Barrington	Gutenberg	Harris
Great Britain	Guthrie	Harrisburg
Great Falls	Guy	Harrison
Great Neck	Hackensack	Harrisonburg
Greece	Haddonfield	Hartford
Greeley	Haddon Heights	Hartman
Green	Hagerstown	Hartsville
Green Bay	Haggerty	Harvey
Greenfield	Haiti	Hasbrouck Heights
Greensboro	Halifax	Hastings
Greensburg	Hall	Hattiesburg
Greenville	Hamburg	Havana
Greenwood	Hamilton	Haverford
Gregory	Hammond	Haverstraw
Grenada	Hampton	Havre
Greta	Hancock	Hawaii
Gretchen	Hanford	Hawthorne
Gretna	Hannah	Hays
Griffin	Hannibal	Hayward
Griffiths	Hanover	Hazard
Grinnell	Hans	Healy
Griselda	Hansen	Hector
Gross	Hanson	Hedwig

Helen	Hoffman	Hudson
Helena	Holdenville	Hugh
Heloise	Holland	Hughes
Hempstead	Hollywood	Hugo
Henderson	Holmes	Huldah
Henrietta	Holt	Humboldt
Henry	Holyoke	Humphrey
Herbert	Homer	Hungary
Herkimer	Homestead	Hunter
Herman	Homewood	Huntington
Hermosa Beach	Honduras	Huntsville
Herrin	Honesdale	Huron
Hester	Hong Kong	Hutchinson
Hezekiah	Honolulu	Hyattsville
Hibbing	Hoover	Iceland
Hickory	Hope	Ichabod
Higgins	Hopewell	Ida
Highland Park	Hopkins	Idaho
High Point	Hopkinsville	Idaho Falls
Hilda	Horace	Ignatius
Hill	Horatio	Illinois
Hillsboro	Hornel	Imogene
Hillsdale	Hortense	Independence
Hillside	Horton	India
Hingham	Hosea	Indiana
Hinsdale	Hot Springs	Indianapolis
Hinton	Houston	Inglewood
Hiram	Howard	Iola
Hobart	Howell	Iowa
Hoboken	Hubbs	Iowa City
Hodges	Hubert	Ipswich

307

Ira	Jamaica	Joan
Iran	James	Job
Iraq	Jamestown	Jocelin
Ireland	Jane	Jock
Irene	Janesville	Joel
Iris	Janet	John
Irma	Janice	Johnson
Iron Mountain	Japan	Johnston
Ironton	Jared	Johnstown
Ironwood	Jarvis	Joliet
Irving	Jason	Jonah
Irvington	Jasper	Jonas
Irwin	Jean	Jonathan
Isaac	Jeannette	Jones
Isabel	Jefferson	Jonesboro
Isadora	Jeffersonville	Joplin
Ishpeming	Jeffrey	Joseph
Isidore	Jemima	Joyce
Isolde	Jenkins	Judah
Israel	Jenkintown	Jude
Istanbul	Jennifer	Judith
Italy	Jennings	Julia
Ithaca	Jenny	Julian
Ivan	Jeremiah	Juliana
Ivy	Jerome	Juliet
Jabez	Jersey City	Julius
Jack	Jerusalem	June
Jackson	Jessamine	Junius
Jacksonville	Jesse	Justin
Jacobs	Jessica	Justina
Jacqueline	Jessie	Kabul

Kalamazoo	Keyport	Lake City
Kalispell	Keyser	Lake Forest
Kane	Key West	Lakeland
Kankakee	Kharkov	Lake Wales
Kansas	Kilgore	Lakewood
Kansas City	Kimball	Lake Worth
Karen	King	Lambert
Karl	Kingsford	Lancaster
Kate	Kingston	Lancelot
Katharine	Kingsville	Lanett
Kathleen	Kinston	Lansdale
Kawanee	Kirksville	Lansdowne
Kearny	Kirkwood	Lansford
Keene	Kittanning	Lansing
Keith	Kitty	La Paz
Kelly	Klamath Falls	Lapeer
Kelso	Klein	La Porte
Kelvin	Knight	Laramie
Kendallville	Knox	Larchmont
Kenmore	Knoxville	Laredo
Kennedy	Kokomo	Larksville
Kenneth	Korea	Lars
Kennett	Laban	Larson
Kenosha	Lacey	La Salle
Kent	Lackawanna	Las Cruces
Kenton	Laconia	Las Vegas
Kentucky	La Crosse	Latrobe
Keokuk	La Grande	Latvia
Kerr	Lafayette	Laughlin
Kerrville	La Junta	Laura
Kester	Lake Charles	Laurel

Laurens	Leroy	Llewellyn
Laurinburg	Leslie	Lloyd
Lavinia	Lester	Lockhart
Lawrence	Letitia	Lock Haven
Lawrenceville	Lettice	Lockport
Lawton	Levy	Lodi
Lazarus	Lewis	Logan
Lead	Lewiston	Logansport
Leah	Lewistown	Lois
Leander	Lexington	Lola
Leavenworth	Libby	Lombard
Lebanon	Liberia	London
Lederer	Liechtenstein	Long
Lee	Lillian	Long Beach
Leeds	Lilly	Long Branch
Lehighton	Lima	Longview
Lehman	Limon	Lorain
Leipsig	Lincoln	Lorenzo
Lelia	Linden	Loretta
Le Mars	Lindstrom	Lorinda
Lemuel	Linton	Los Angeles
Lena	Lionel	Louis
Leningrad	Lisa	Louisa
Lenoir	Lisbon	Louise
Leo	Litchfield	Louisiana
Leominster	Lithuania	Louisville
Leon	Little Falls	Loveland
Leonard	Little Rock	Lowell
Leonia	Liverpool	Lubbock
Leonora	Livingston	Lucinda
Leopold	Livingstone	Lucius

Lucretia	Mahoney	Marilla
Lucy	Maine	Marinette
Ludington	Malden	Marion
Ludlow	Malone	Marlboro
Luella	Malvern	Marlin
Lufkin	Malverne	Marquette
Luke	Manchester	Marseilles
Lumberton	Mandan	Marshall
Luther	Mandy	Marshalltown
Luxembourg	Manhattan	Marshfield
Luzerne	Manila	Martha
Lydia	Manistee	Martin
Lyle	Manistique	Martinez
Lynbrook	Manitoba	Martinsburg
Lynch	Manitowoc	Martinsville
Lynchburg	Mankato	Maryville
Lyndhurst	Mannheim	Mason
Lynn	Manuel	Mason City
Lynwood	Manzala	Massachusetts
Lyons	Maple Heights	Massena
Mabel	Maplewood	Massillon
Mack	Marblehead	Mathilda
Madeline	Marcella	Matthew
Madge	Marcellus	Mattoon
Madison	Marcia	Maud
Madisonville	Marcus	Maurice
Madrid	Margaret	Maximilian
Mae	Marguery	Maxwell
Magdalene	Marian	May
Maguire	Marianna	Maynard
Mahanoy City	Marietta	Maysville

311

Mayville	Menominee	Minden
Maywood	Mercedes	Mineola
McAdoo	Mercy	Minersville
McCabe	Meriden	Minerva
McCann	Merrill	Mingo Junction
McCarthy	Mesa	Minneapolis
McCauley	Methuen	Minnesota
McComb	Metuchen	Minnie
McCook	Mexico	Minot
McCormack	Meyer	Miranda
McDonald	Miami	Miriam
McGregor	Micah	Mission
McIntosh	Michael	Mississippi
McKee	Michigan	Missoula
McKeesport	Middleboro	Missouri
McKees Rocks	Middletown	Mitchell
McKenzie	Midland	Moberly
McKinney	Milan	Mobile
McLean	Mildred	Modesto
McLeod	Miles	Moira
McMillan	Miles City	Moline
McPherson	Milford	Monaca
Meadville	Milicent	Monessen
Mechanicsburg	Millburn	Monica
Mechanicville	Millbury	Monmouth
Medford	Milledgeville	Monroe
Melbourne	Miller	Monrovia
Melissa	Millvale	Montague
Melrose	Millville	Montana
Memphis	Milton	Montclair
Menasha	Milwaukee	Montebello

312

Monterey	Munich	Nathan
Montevideo	Murdock	Nathaniel
Montgomery	Murfreesboro	Natick
Montpelier	Muriel	Naugatuck
Montreal	Murphy	Nazareth
Moore	Murphysboro	Neal
Mooresville	Murray	Nebraska
Moorhead	Muscatine	Needham
Morgan	Muskegon	Neenah
Morgantown	Myers	Negaunee
Morocco	Myra	Nehemiah
Morris	Myrtle	Nellie
Morrison	Naaman	Nelson
Morristown	Nampa	Nelsonville
Morrisville	Nancy	Neptune
Morse	Nanking	Nerissa
Mortimer	Nannette	Netherlands
Moscow	Nanticoke	Nevada
Moses	Nanty-Glo	New Albany
Moultrie	Naomi	Newark
Moundsville	Napa	New Bedford
Mount Airy	Naperville	New Bern
Mount Carmel	Naples	Newberry
Mount Clemens	Napoleon	New Boston
Mount Kisco	Nash	New Braunfels
Mount Lebanon	Nashua	New Brighton
Mount Oliver	Nashville	New Britain
Mount Pleasant	Natal	New Brunswick
Mount Vernon	Natalie	Newburgh
Muncie	Natchez	Newburyport
Munhall	Natchitoches	New Castle

Newfoundland	North Adams	Oelwein
New Hampshire	Northampton	Ogden
New Haven	North Bergen	Ogdensburg
New Jersey	North Braddock	Ohio
New Kensington	Northbridge	Oil City
New London	North Carolina	Oklahoma
New Mexico	North Chicago	Oklahoma City
New Orleans	North Dakota	Okmulgee
Newport	North Platte	Old Forge
Newport News	Norwalk	Old Town
New Rochelle	Norway	Olean
Newton	Norwich	Olga
New Ulm	Norwood	Olive
New York	Nottingham	Oliver
New Zealand	Nova Scotia	Olney
Niagara Falls	Nuremberg	Olsen
Nicaragua	Nutley	Olson
Nicholas	Nyack	Olympia
Niles	Oakland	Olyphant
Niles Center	Oakmont	Omaha
Nina	Oak Park	Oneida
Noah	Oakwood	O'Neil
Noel	Obadiah	Oneonta
Nogales	O'Brien	Ontario
Nolan	Ocala	Opelika
Nora	O'Connor	Opelousas
Norfolk	Oconto	Ophelia
Norma	Octavia	Orange
Normal	Octavius	Orangeburg
Norman	Odessa	Oregon
Norristown	O'Donnell	Orlando

Oscar	Parkersburg	Peoria
Oshkosh	Park Ridge	Percival
Oskaloosa	Parma	Percy
Oslo	Parsons	Perry
Osmund	Pasadena	Perth Amboy
Ossining	Pascagoula	Peru
Oswald	Passaic	Petaluma
Oswego	Patchogue	Peter
Ottawa	Paterson	Petersburg
Otto	Patience	Petersen
Ottumwa	Patricia	Peterson
Owego	Patrick	Petoskey
Owen	Paul	Phelps
Owensboro	Paula	Philadelphia
Owosso	Paulina	Philander
Oxnard	Pauline	Philip
Packard	Paulsboro	Philippa
Paducah	Pawtucket	Philippine Islands
Painesville	Peabody	Phillips
Palestine	Peale	Phillipsburg
Palmer	Pearl	Phineas
Palmerton	Pearson	Phoebe
Palmyra	Peekskill	Phoenix
Palo Alto	Peggy	Phoenixville
Pamela	Pekin	Phyllis
Pampa	Pelham	Piedmont
Panama	Pendleton	Pierce
Pansy	Penns Grove	Pine Bluff
Paraguay	Pennsylvania	Pitcairn
Paris	Penn Yan	Pitman
Parker	Pensacola	Pittsburgh

315

Pittsfield
Pittston
Pius
Plainfield
Plains
Plainview
Plant City
Plaquemine
Plattsburg
Pleasantville
Plymouth
Pocatello
Poland
Polly
Ponca City
Pontiac
Portage
Portales
Port Angeles
Port Arthur
Port Chester
Porter
Porterville
Port Huron
Portia
Port Jervis
Portland
Portsmouth
Portugal
Potter
Pottstown

Pottsville
Poughkeepsie
Powell
Powers
Prague
Pratt
Prescott
Presque Isle
Price
Prichard
Princeton
Priscilla
Providence
Provo
Prudence
Pueblo
Puerto Rico
Pulaski
Putnam
Puyallup
Quakertown
Quebec
Queensland
Quincy
Quinn
Quito
Rachel
Racine
Radford
Rahway
Raleigh

Ralph
Ramona
Randall
Randolph
Rankin
Rapid City
Raton
Ravenna
Ray
Raymond
Reading
Reba
Rebecca
Red Bank
Redlands
Red Oak
Red Wing
Redwood City
Regina
Reginald
Reid
Reidsville
Reinhardt
Reno
Renshaw
Rensselaer
Reuben
Revere
Rex
Reynolds
Rhea

316

Rhinelander	Rocky Mount	Russia
Rhoda	Roderick	Ruston
Rhode Island	Roger	Ruth
Rhodes	Roland	Rutherford
Richard	Rolla	Rutland
Richfield	Rollo	Ryan
Richman	Romania	Rye
Richmond	Rome	Ryerson
Richwood	Romola	Saco
Ridgefield	Roosevelt	Sacramento
Ridgeway	Rosa	Saginaw
Ridgewood	Rosalind	Saguenay
Riga	Roscoe	St. Albans
Riley	Roselle	St. Augustine
Rio de Janeiro	Rosemary	St. Bernard
Rita	Roseville	St. Charles
River Rouge	Ross	St. Clair
Riverside	Rossville	St. Cloud
Roanoke	Roswell	St. John
Robbins	Rotterdam	St. Johnsbury
Robbinsdale	Rowena	St. Joseph
Robert	Roy	St. Louis
Robertson	Royal Oak	St. Marys
Robinson	Ruby	St. Paul
Robstown	Rudolph	St. Peter
Rochester	Rufus	St. Petersburg
Rockford	Rumford Falls	Salamanca
Rock Island	Rupert	Salem
Rockland	Rushville	Salina
Rock Springs	Rusk	Salinas
Rockville	Russell	Salisbury

Salome	Santa Monica	Seattle
Salt Lake City	Santa Paula	Secaucus
Sampson	Santa Rosa	Sedalia
Samuel	Santiago	Selma
San Angelo	Sapulpa	Seminole
San Anselmo	Sarah	Seneca Falls
San Antonio	Saranac Lake	Serena
San Benito	Sarasota	Seth
San Bernardino	Saratoga Springs	Seville
San Bruno	Saugus	Seward
Sanders	Saul	Sewickley
San Diego	Sault Ste. Marie	Sexton
Sand Springs	Saunders	Seymour
Sandusky	Savannah	Shaker Heights
San Fernando	Sawyer	Shamokin
Sanford	Sayre	Shanghai
San Francisco	Sayreville	Sharon
San Gabriel	Scarsdale	Sharp
San Jose	Schenectady	Sharpsburg
San Leandro	Schmidt	Sharpsville
San Luis Obispo	Schneider	Shaw
San Marcos	Schroeder	Shawnee
San Marino	Schultz	Shea
San Mateo	Schuyler	Sheboygan
San Rafael	Schwartz	Sheffield
Santa Ana	Scotia	Sheila
Santa Barbara	Scotland	Shelby
Santa Clara	Scott	Shelbyville
Santa Cruz	Scottdale	Sheldon
Santa Fe	Scottsbluff	Shenandoah
Santa Maria	Scranton	Sheridan

Sherman	Somerset	Stalingrad
Sherwood	Somerville	Stamford
Shippensburg	Somersworth	Stanford
Shirley	Sonora	Stanley
Shoemaker	Sophia	State College
Shorewood	Sophronia	Statesboro
Shreveport	Sorensen	Statesville
Siam	South Africa	Staunton
Sibyl	South Amboy	Steelton
Sicily	South America	Stella
Sidney	South Bend	Stephen
Siegal	South Boston	Sterling
Siegfried	Southbridge	Steubenville
Sikeston	South Carolina	Stevens
Silas	South Dakota	Stewart
Silvanus	South Hadley	Stillwater
Silvester	Southampton	Stockholm
Silvia	Southington	Stockton
Simmons	South Orange	Stone
Simon	South River	Stoneham
Simpson	Spain	Storm Lake
Sinclair	Sparks	Stoughton
Singapore	Sparta	Stowe
Sioux City	Spartanburg	Stratford
Sioux Falls	Spencer	Straus
Skinner	Spokane	Streator
Sloan	Sprague	Stroudsburg
Smith	Springfield	Struthers
Snyder	Spring Valley	Stuart
Soloman	Stacey	Sturgeon Bay
Solvay	Stafford	Sturgis

Stuttgart	Tampa	Tifton
Sudan	Tampico	Tilda
Suffolk	Tarboro	Timothy
Sullivan	Tarentum	Tipton
Summit	Tarrytown	Titus
Sumner	Tasmania	Titusville
Sumter	Taunton	Tobiah
Sunbury	Taylor	Tokyo
Superior	Taylorville	Toledo
Susan	Teaneck	Tonawanda
Swampscott	Temple	Tony
Swansea	Tenafly	Toole
Sweden	Tennessee	Topeka
Sweetwater	Terence	Toronto
Swift	Terre Haute	Torrance
Swissvale	Terrel	Torrington
Switzerland	Terry	Toulouse
Sybil	Texarkana	Trenton
Sydney	Texas	Trieste
Sylvanus	Texas City	Trinidad
Sylvester	Thaddeus	Tripoli
Sylvia	Thalia	Troy
Syracuse	Thea	Truman
Syria	The Hague	Tuckahoe
Tabitha	Theodore	Tucson
Tacoma	Theodora	Tulane
Taft	Theresa	Tulsa
Talladega	Thomas	Tunis
Tallahassee	Thomaston	Tupelo
Tallulah	Thomasville	Turin
Tamaqua	Tiffin	Turkey

Turner	Vance	Waddington
Tuscaloosa	Vanderlip	Wadsworth
Tuscumbia	Van Dyke	Wakefield
Twin Falls	Van Horn	Wales
Tyler	Van Wert	Walker
Tyrone	Vatican City	Wallace
Ukraine	Vaughan	Walla Walla
Ulrich	Venezuela	Wallingford
Ulysses	Venice	Wallington
Underhill	Ventnor City	Walpole
Underwood	Vera Cruz	Walsenburg
Union	Vermont	Walsh
Union City	Vernon	Walter
United Kingdom	Verona	Waltham
United States	Veronica	Ward
Upland	Vicksburg	Ware
Upton	Victor	Warren
Urban	Victoria	Warrensburg
Urbana	Villa Park	Warsaw
Uriah	Vincennes	Warwick
Ursula	Vincent	Washington
Uruguay	Vineland	Waterbury
Utah	Vienna	Waterloo
Utica	Viola	Watertown
Vail	Violet	Waterville
Valdosta	Virgil	Watervliet
Valentine	Virginia	Watson
Valeria	Visalia	Watsonville
Valley City	Vivian	Waukegan
Valley Stream	Wabash	Waukesha
Valparaiso	Waco	Waupun

Wausau	Weymouth	Winona
Waverly	Wheaton	Winooski
Waxahachie	Wheeling	Winslow
Waycross	White	Winsted
Waynesboro	White Plains	Winston-Salem
Weatherford	Whiting	Winter
Webb City	Whitman	Winthrop
Webster	Whittier	Winton
Welch	Wichita	Wisconsin
Wellesley	Wilbur	Woburn
Wellington	Wildwood	Wolf
Wellsburg	Wilfred	Wood
Wellston	Wilkes-Barre	Woodbridge
Wellsville	Wilkinsburg	Woodbury
Wenatchee	Willard	Woodland
Wesley	William	Wood River
West Allis	Williamson	Woodruff
West Bend	Williamsport	Woodstock
Westbrook	Willimantic	Woodward
West Chester	Williston	Woonsocket
Westerly	Willmar	Wooster
Westfield	Wilmerding	Worcester
West Haven	Wilmette	Worthington
West New York	Wilmington	Wyandotte
Weston	Wilson	Wyoming
West Orange	Winchester	Xenia
West Point	Windber	Yakima
West View	Winfield	Yankton
West Virginia	Winifred	Yates
Westwood	Winnetka	Yazoo City
West York	Winnipeg	Yokohama

322

Yonkers	Ypsilanti	Yvonne
York	Yucatan	Zanesville
Young	Yugoslavia	Zenobia
Youngstown	Yuma	Zion

PART THREE
ABBREVIATIONS

Some expressions are dictated and transcribed almost exclusively in abbreviated form, such as *f.o.b.* Some expressions may be dictated and transcribed either in full or in the form of initials, such as *A.C.* or *alternating current*. The following list contains 72 such expressions with a legible shorthand outline for each set of initials.

AAF	Army Air Forces	
ABC	American Broadcasting Company	
A.C.	alternating current	
A.D.	*anno Domini*	
AEC	Atomic Energy Commission	
A.F. of L.	American Federation of Labor	
A.L.P.	American Labor Party	
a.m.	ante meridiem	
A.M.A.	American Medical Association	
A.O.L.	absent over leave	
APO	Army Post Office	
A.S.C.A.P.	American Society of Composers, Authors, and Publishers	
ASTP	Army Specialized Training Program	

A.W.O.L.	absent without leave	
B.B.A.	Bachelor of Business Administration	
B.B.C.	British Broadcasting Corporation	
B.I.S.	Bank for International Settlements	
BLS	Bureau of Labor Statistics	
B.t.u.	British thermal unit	
CBI	China, Burma, India	
CBS	Columbia Broadcasting System	
cc.	cubic centimeters	
c.i.f.	cost, insurance, and freight	
C.I.O.	Congress of Industrial Organizations	
C.O.D.	collect on delivery	
C.P.A.	Certified Public Accountant	
C.S.R.	Certified Shorthand Reporter	
c.w.o.	cash with order	
D.A.	District Attorney	
D.A.R.	Daughters of the American Revolution	
D.C.	direct current	
D.D.S.	Doctor of Dental Surgery	
DP	displaced person	

DX	distance	
E. & O.E.	errors and omissions excepted	
Ed. D.	Doctor of Education	
E.Q.	educational quotient	
ERP	European Recovery Program	
ETO	European Theater of Operation	
FCC	Federal Communications Commission	
FDIC	Federal Deposit Insurance Corporation	
FM	frequency modulation	
f.o.b.	free on board	
FPC	Federal Power Commission	
FSA	Federal Security Agency	
FTC	Federal Trade Commission	
GHQ	General Headquarters	
HOLC	Home Owners Loan Corporation	
ICC	Interstate Commerce Commission	
I.L.O.	International Labor Organization	
IQ	intelligence quotient	
ITO	International Trade Organization	
M.D.	Doctor of Medicine	

NBC	National Broadcasting Company
N.E.A.	National Education Association
NLRB	National Labor Relations Board
OPA	Office of Price Administration
OSS	Office of Strategic Services
PBX	private branch exchange
p.m.	post meridiem
P.S.	postscript
P.T.A.	Parent-Teacher Association
q.v.	which see
R.F.D.	Rural Free Delivery
ROTC	Reserve Officers' Training Corps
r.p.m.	revolutions per minute
TNT	trinitrotoluene
TVA	Tennessee Valley Authority
USES	United States Employment Service
VA	Veterans' Administration
W.F.T.U.	World Federation of Trade Unions
WPA	Works Progress Administration